AMERICAN WATERS

For Josh Feigenbaum, because we all need a fishing buddy

AMERICAN WATERS

Fly-Fishing Journeys of a Native Son

Peter Kaminsky

Stewart, Tabori & Chang · New York

Published in 2005 by
Stewart, Tabori & Chang
115 West 18th Street
New York, NY 10011
www.abramsbooks.com

Library of Congress Cataloging-in-Publication Data
Kaminsky, Peter.
American waters: the fly-fishing journeys of a native son / Peter Kaminsky.
      p. cm.
Includes index.
ISBN 1-58479-471-2
1. Fly fishing—North America—anecdotes. I. Title.

SH462.K36 2005
799.12'4'097—dc22   2005013272

Designer: Julie Hoffer
Production Manager: Jane Searle

The text of this book was composed in Mrs. Eaves and Hoefler Text.

Printed in China

10 9 8 7 6 5 4 3 2 1

First Printing

Stewart, Tabori & Chang is a subsidiary of

LA MARTINIÈRE

Acknowledgments

In order not to forget *anyone*, first I would like to acknowledge *everyone* I ever fished with, or with whom I talked about fishing, or who wrote about fishing. Fly, plug, or bait—I learned from them all. To Leslie Stoker, for telling me, "Go ahead, make it personal, it's your story." Julie Hoffer has done a lovely job designing a book on a subject about which she knows hardly anything, but her soulful intelligence meant that she got it all in a heartbeat. Jennifer Eiss, for making sure that nothing fell between the cracks. Lisa Queen, my agent and cheer-leader, and, with her, everyone at LQL. Mark Horowitz, for reading the manuscript. Tom Akstens, as always, for making sure there were fewer mistakes after he looked things over. To John Randolph, for recommending the services of Jay Nichols, who carefully and expertly edited the text.

The outstanding photographers who made their finest work available are hereby thanked, both for their pictures and their generosity in letting us afford their work. Among them are old friends Tom Akstens, Keith Meyers, Richard Franklin, Larry Aiuppy, Allan Finkelman, and Jim Levison. The great Valentine Atkinson, who I have been lucky enough to have supply me photos for stories over the years. A new buddy and true master, Andy Anderson. The artful Ed Wargin. Tosh Brown and Dusan Smetana, who were recommended by Sid Evans as "the best in the business." Soc Clay, too, for a particularly lyrical shot. Tom Montgomery, who came late but well supplied to the party, and Sam Talarico, for his one-of-a-kind take on things. Glenn Wolff, who always comes through with his drawings. Paul Dixon, for making Montauk a magic place. Steve Sautner and Joe Shastay, for turning me on to fishing in the Big Apple. Nick Lyons, the Scoutmaster to my generation of angling writers and the guy who recommended me to the *New York Times*. Susan B. Adams, who has looked after outdoors writers in the Sports Section as if they were family, which she certainly is to us. And Melinda, who in all these years only complained once about my running away to fish, and that was on Thanksgiving morning, when I was supposed to help make dinner. I made it back in time, and I believe the turkey was improved by my absence.

TABLE OF CONTENTS

The pleasant'st angling is to see the fish

Cut with her golden oars the silver stream,

And greedily devour the treacherous bait . . .

Shakespeare, *Much Ado about Nothing*

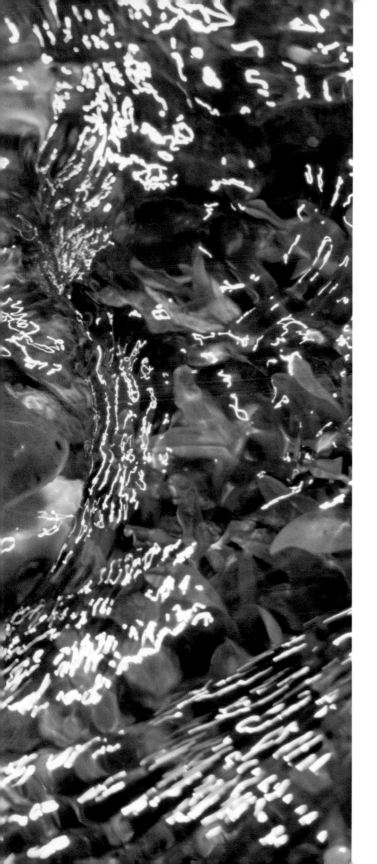

HOME WATER

BIRTH OF A FLY FISHERMAN

I wasn't born a fly fisherman. Somehow I made it through twenty-five years of life in nearly total ignorance of fly-fishing. I think it would be accurate to say I was reborn as a fly-fisherman, or even that I was born again. I don't know how else to describe the feelings of pleasure, timelessness, grace, and beauty that fly-fishing instills in me. Fly-fishing put me in touch with the world, and at the same time it put me in touch with myself.

People feel this way about golf, or fine wine, or painting, or reading poetry, or meditating under a banyan tree, so I am not proposing that fly-fishing is the one true path to fulfillment; but for me it sure is.

"Why fly-fishing?" I am often asked.

I have no good answer. If you were to ask me why I liked anything else, it would be easier to come up with a reply; I would measure it against my feelings for this pastime. Fly-fishing, like food or family, is one of those things that just is. How do I know that? I know it in the same way that you know any deep truth. Certain truths are, as Tom Jefferson said, "self-evident."

Self-evident, yes, but first I had to pick up a fly rod. The year was 1974. After a couple of years of driving a New York City cab, and a few more in grad school, I found myself as an editor at *National Lampoon*. You could not dream up a less outdoorsy place.

That winter, I went to the Florida Keys for vacation. I didn't know then that the Keys are a great fishing mecca. I thought they were warm like the Bahamas, and I could drive there after visiting my grandfather in Miami Beach. I was wrong. That winter, it was cold all around the Gulf of Mexico: 39 degrees in Havana. Swimming and lying around on the beach were out of the question, so I drove along U.S. 1 looking for something to do.

And then I saw a sign. Not a sign from the heavens, although it might just as well have been, but a road-side sign: "Red Snapper All Day $19."

On a whim, I went up to the dock, where a boat full of hopeful fishermen was about to weigh anchor.

"Got room?" I asked.

"Sure," the mate answered, and I jumped on board. When we got out to the reef, I dropped my baited hook into the blue-green water and soon I felt a tug. Apparently my offering had landed right under the nose of a 35-pound grouper.

At that life-changing moment, I was hooked on fishing.

Still, I didn't know a fly-rod from a hot rod. That part of my education began the next winter in the Yucatan. The highly recommended "unspoiled Mayan village" where I had booked a room proved to be a little too Club Med for me, so I kept going south, past the serene, sun-washed pyramids of Tulum. Twenty miles farther on, I saw a sign for "Boca Paila, Fishing Lodge." On one side of the road lay a giant lagoon with half a dozen Boston Whalers riding at anchor. On the other side, gentle breakers rode over an offshore reef where the water turned from green to blue. Thatched cottages lined the shore.

It was lunchtime and the proprietor, Tony Gonzalez, invited me in for tequila with fresh-squeezed grapefruit juice, broiled shrimp and rock lobsters, homemade tortillas, and guacamole. The lodgers totaled eight, all of them American, all of them middle-aged, all of them in khaki pants and shirts—the kind that have been washed a lot and probably never ironed. They couldn't have been friendlier. I unpacked the car and moved in for a week.

I spent six great days catching bonefish on spinning tackle. These creatures ran like crazy, which is what their DNA impelled them to do as soon as they sensed danger. When you live in 3 feet of water, a good defense from predators is the ability to take off like turbocharged lightning at any sign of trouble.

For the first time, or at least the first time that it registered with me, I saw people with fly rods.

While this activity seemed to absorb my camp mates, to me, it looked like an angling version of badminton. I didn't pay it much mind, at least consciously. Things started to change, though, soon after my return to New York, when I met the friend of a mutual friend for a drink. "She loves to fish," my buddy said.

Marsha Norman—pretty, vivacious, and very southern—soon became a pal. Her husband, Geoff, was an editor and columnist at *Esquire*. He was also an ex–Green Beret, a lifelong outdoorsman, and a terrific writer. His clean, yet personal sentences are still a model for me when I catch myself running on.

"We're going up to the Catskills to fly-fish on the Beaverkill this weekend, wanna come?" he asked, and I accepted. So we trooped upstate to a damp and dark streamside motel that could well have served as a center for the study of mildew.

After we dropped off our duffels, Geoff led the way to a beautiful pool on the Beaverkill.

"I was here one day last summer," he recalled. "There were clouds of Tricos [the smallest mayfly] blowing off the water. Nothing much happening, and

then the air got really thick, just before a thunderstorm. Black clouds moved in and, in the stillness, the pool came alive. I caught fish after fish. Nice ones."

Geoff waded in and fired off a cast that shot across the stream like a tracer bullet, but the fish weren't interested.

"Too cold," he said. We walked across the old bridge just downstream from our parking spot. We stopped on the bridge, as fishermen always do, looking for trout finning in the current. There wasn't much to see. The stream was deserted except for one angler, a silver-haired man who sent out cast after cast, straight, true, and quite long. On this otherwise fishless afternoon he caught a half dozen fish. He even took one out of a current pocket in front of a bridge abutment, which I later learned always held a big and uncatchable brown trout.

The white-haired fisherman was good. We watched him till he stopped and then, when he too crossed the bridge, I offered him a swig from my flask of Jack Daniel's.

"You're really good," I said. "We enjoyed watching you. What's your name?"

"Doug Swisher," he said. It meant nothing to me but got a raised eyebrow from Geoff. Swisher, it turned out, is one of modern fly-fishing's stars and the coauthor (with Carl Richards) of the seminal work *Selective Trout*. He had come to the Beaverkill to give a three-day casting clinic.

"Can I still enroll?" I inquired.

I signed up and spent the next three days learning the mechanics of casting and the extremely valuable variations of the basic cast that informed all of my fishing in the years to come. While, to an outsider, casting may look rather difficult, I came to believe, and continue to believe, that if a new angler spends a few days learning to cast, he or she is ready to catch fish. Perhaps not with the finesse or the distance of a veteran, but good enough.

And so I cast . . . and cast . . . and cast. I loved the motion, the unfurling of the line, the snap as it straightened, and the descent of the leader and fly,

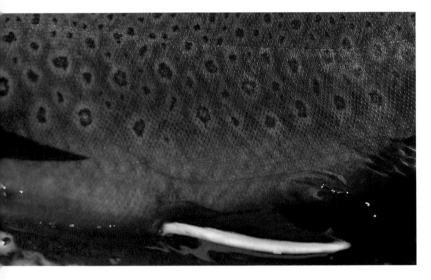

"light as a snowflake," as the old casting books often put it. I spent hours with my rod up on Sheeps Meadow in Brooklyn's Prospect Park. Come the weekend, whenever I wasn't on the water I was out on the lawn of the house I rented by a trout stream in Mt. Tremper, New York. I found the long, elegant movement of the line totally captivating. As for my hours on the stream, I couldn't get enough of them.

Fly fishing proved to be just the right balance to life at *Lampoon*, which was getting a bit weird and druggy in the late 1970s. When I finally left the magazine in early '78, I resolved to make my living writing about fishing. Since then, fishing has taken me to the prettiest places—from the tip of Tierra del Fuego to the edge of the Arctic, from the bountiful riptides of Montauk Point to the spring creeks of Montana. It took me to places in America that a New York City guy would never have visited were it not for fishing assignments. Where many other fishing writers were looking to get sent to the legendary—and more expensive—angling destinations of the world, I was equally happy to spend a week floating the meandering rivers of the Ozarks, or jigging with a sinking line for walleye in northern Minnesota, or tossing crickets at fat bluegill with a peach millionaire on his Georgia farm. I met cops, firemen, race-car drivers, football coaches, refugee princes, carpenters, poets, assembly line workers, ski bums, grade-school teachers, and guitar players.

Fishing introduced me to my own country in ways I might never have known. In this volume I hope to share my journeys around the fishingest country on earth. Every chapter is a journey. Some are to the most remote spots in America, from Native American lands deep in the heart of the Everglades to streams at 10,000 feet and 50 miles from the nearest road. Some are no farther than the Brooklyn waterfront, a block from my home. Some brought me to the feet of the great masters of angling: I call them Lords of the Fly. Still others brought me to the kitchens of some of the greatest chefs in the world. This book, then, is an all-American highlight reel of the pastime that angling's Obi Wan Kenobe, the immortal Lee Wulff, called "This wonderful sport."

FIRST LOVE:
The Esopus

———◆———

The only thing I can compare to the first river you fish is your first love affair. Consider the symptoms of puppy love and fledgling angling. First, when you are not on the river, all you can think of is being there. Second, when you are there, the feeling is intense and ultimately fleeting, so that when it is time to go, all you can do is muster a generalized "So soon!!?" Third, when you get to the stream, arriving "with wings on your feet," you are in a fevered rush to get into your fishing outfit, instead of out of it, which may be the principal difference between a love affair and a fishing session. But in both cases the hurried urgency to get down to the business at hand is irresistible. Fourth, after you have left you cannot wait to return as soon as possible. Fifth, in this stage of your education there is no intimacy that is too extreme: you want to know and to experience absolutely everything about the object of your desire. Sixth, in answer to the question, "Why are you so in love?" there is no answer other than, "What else is there?"

Seventh, eighth, ninth, tenth . . . and on and on; the reasons are endless and, in the final analysis, meaningless, because you don't need any reason apart from the fact that you are contented when you are there and in a state of longing when you are not.

For me, that first river love affair is a stream in the Catskills called Esopus Creek. Even now the word *Esopus* jumps off the page at me the way my own name does. It was one of the home rivers of American fly-fishing. Theodore Gordon, the founding father of modern dry-fly fishing, knew it well. So did Lee Wulff—the first master angler of modern times (or maybe the last one of the classic era). Right across from the little house I rented on one of its tributaries, the Native American guide and legendary fly-tier Ray Smith once lived. Down the road was Dick Cahill's Rainbow Lodge and, to dispel any confusion about what kind of rainbow it was named after, the sign in front featured a fat rainbow trout, its muscular body arched like a crescent as it sought to free itself from a fly lodged in its lip. The first issue of *Fly Fisherman* magazine was laid out in the living room at Cahill's. Preston Jennings had spent the early 1930s researching his immortal study, *A Book of Trout Flies*, just down the road from my house at the confluence of the Esopus and the Little Beaverkill, one of many Catskill rivers bearing this name owing, no doubt, to the thriving population of beavers in the region. Jennings documented the major mayfly hatches and customized fly patterns that would work on the river. In the decades that followed, other authors, such as Art Flick, Ernie Schwiebert, Al Caucci, and Doug Swisher, repeated this exercise on other rivers. As practical handbooks, if you had no other instructors than these, your trout-fishing education would be well taken care of.

The Esopus benefited from the outflow of Schoharie Reservoir. When summer's heat and low water rendered other rivers unfishable for trout, a cool bottom release was delivered into the Esopus by a long tunnel that issued from beneath the mountains in Allaben. Because of this cool water, rainbow trout thrived in the Esopus. In fact they did so well that there was no need for the state to stock the stream. Huge rainbows spent the summer gorging on alewive herring in Ashokan Reservoir, and come spring these predators would ascend the Esopus and its tributaries to spawn. These beautiful wild fish fought delightfully in the rushing current.

I learned to wade in the Esopus. I am glad I did it when I did, because if I had waited until I first fished the brook trout flowages of Labrador, or the Yellowstone and Madison of Montana, you could bet money that I would have gone ass over teakettle many more times than turned out to be the case. As I think about it, I can only recall four times that I actually slipped and fell into a stream. To fish the Esopus you had to be able to handle strong current and slippery rocks.

I felt that I knew every stone in the river, from Allaben down to the reservoir. It got so that no matter where I was—even back home in New York—if I looked at the sun I could tell you exactly where the line of shadow fell on each pool and where it would be in an hour. I learned, after much futile casting, to distinguish between a splashy rise to a caddis and a more purposeful mayfly take. The former would get my attention but rarely signaled a good trout, or, when it did, the trout would be so desultory and fickle in its feeding that it wasn't worth a cast.

Most everything I know, I first started to learn on the Esopus. How to cast into the wind, or with a cross wind, or a howling tail wind. How to throw slack into a line so that the fly gained an extra half second of drag-free float (which invariably made the difference).

The Esopus was especially lovely at first light on July mornings when the fog hung heavy on the cool surface of the river. I remember one such morning when I was in my late twenties. My brother, Bob, who is not an angler, wanted to get a picture of me fishing. We were out the door before 5 A.M. We drove over the Cold Spring Bridge, made a right, and continued past the pavement's end until the dirt road ended. We climbed the old railroad embankment and then crossed a field of wildflowers and berries as we angled toward the river. We followed the sound of rushing water—like the whoosh of a summer breeze late at night. There was a particular spot I wanted to get to at the end of the long pool known as Huddler's Flats, where a channel became a smooth glide. Running water looks almost as if it bulges in such conditions, as if it swells ever so slightly. Five feet out from the bank, when bugs were on the water, there were always feeding trout.

Bob and I sat on the bank, sharing a Clark Bar and smoking cigarettes (it would be another fifteen years or so before I gave them up—the cigarettes, not the candy bars).

Fish started to rise, ever so gently. I watched them for a while and picked one out. I waded into the riffle below the pool, so as not to disturb the water. When I had taken what I judged to be a good casting position, about 30 feet downstream and to the right of the fish, I cast my fly, a #16 Royal Coachman.

Bobby has a picture of me just before I cast. The rod is in my right hand, my landing net hangs behind me, plumb from my vest. I am dragging on my cigarette—a last puff before heading out of the trenches into the fray. The fog is lifting in cottony tufts, and I look like I am rising out of the underworld. The smile on my face is one of anticipated pleasure. In my imagination, at that moment, I saw the rainbow trout on Dick Cahill's sign come to life in the stream.

The fly drifted; the fish took deliberately, unmistakably, and softly. I tightened my line. The fight was nice, I think. I do remember—will never forget—what the fish looked like when it came to hand. Thirteen inches long and fat. A brown trout, with pretty red spots, pastel brown, not deep chocolaty but the lighter color of hot cocoa made with a lot of milk, Nestlé-Quik brown and with the same dark flecks in it.

Funny, isn't it, how after so many years, I can still remember the fly? It's the same way with ball players who can tell you which pitch, in 1964, they smacked for a home run. If things are really important to who you are and what you do, you remember. Come to think of it, I remember that fish much more fully and clearly than I can recall the whole year in which I caught it.

LORDS OF THE FLY: Gino

———◆———

*N*ot *being a lifelong outdoorsman meant that whenever I sought out the greatest anglers, I never did so as* a competitor. I always came with an attitude of "Tell me, from your very knowledgeable vantage point, how it's done."

When you put it that way, people tend to loosen up.

It was fabulous luck that I took up sporting writing at a time when the men who invented modern American fly-fishing were still alive and kicking: McClane, Wulff, Traver, Gingrich. Imagine that you had just begun to study the clarinet and Benny Goodman was your next-door neighbor, and not only could you listen to him play all day, but he'd be glad to answer all of your questions and show you the tricks of the trade. And once you had got swing down pat, suppose Benny moved out and Jimi Hendrix moved in and you went through the whole thing all over again. That was the kind of up-close and personal instruction that my writing brought me.

I learned from the best. But all that being said, I often remind myself that fish don't recognize your angling pedigree. Famous or unfamous, eloquent or tongue-tied, is not as important as how well you cast a fly and whether or not it is the right fly. In this regard, I learned the most by relying on a guy whom I respected, who liked spending time with me, and who was a much better fisherman than I was.

His name was Gene Calogero. I met him on the Esopus as he was casting a dry fly in the flat water above the Mt. Tremper Bridge. The bugs were coming off in good numbers, but the water had that later-summer, bubbly look that rarely produces much activity. I asked Gene what he was casting.

"A White Miller. Closest thing I have to a White Gloved Howdy."

The notion of something called a White Gloved Howdy was intriguing. It was the old-time dry fly that Catskills fishermen used for the *Isonychia*, one of the most prolific hatches on the Esopus.

In the way that these things happen so fortuitously, Gene lived in the cabin just across the street from mine. But it was nestled down by the stream out of sight and I had never seen the occupants. From that moment on we became great friends. Every morning and afternoon we would make our way to the stream.

That first dry-fly evening with Gene turned out to be a rarity. A few years before that, he had given up dry flies in favor of nymphs. He reasoned that surface feeding was more the exception than the rule on the rushing freestone river. He also was heavily influenced by Ernie Schwiebert's *Nymphs*, another of the books born of a stream study that continued the tradition of Jennings's earlier work on the Esopus.

Gene was in the process of tying nymphs for all of the major aquatic insects of the Esopus. He was an art director by trade (on the Ford Mustang account), so he had a creative bent that came out in his flies. His *Isonychia* recipe called for beautiful chestnut-colored fur with a grouse hackle and wild turkey quill for the wing case. For much of the season his rig was a three-fly setup fished down and across. The only difference between his approach and the one favored in the old days was that Gene's

wet flies were modern, match-the-hatch nymphs.

Still, the effect was the same. On point a caddis pupa, then a mayfly, then a stonefly nymph. You would face 45 degrees downstream from the opposite bank, tossing your fly toward shore. The three-fly leader unfurled, and in the slanting light at 9:30 A.M. or 7:30 of a summer's eve, the low sun glinted off the leader. As the flies straightened out on their droppers, the crispy spray flecked the air with gold and silver strokes that hung for a second and then fell to the water like dying fireworks. Such multiple-fly rigs were known, in nineteenth-century parlance, as "a cast." But we all called them "three wets."

The great trance-inducing part of such fishing is that you can do it mindlessly. You cast, fish out your cast, strip in your fly, take a step downstream, and cast again. You begin to get a feeling for exactly which part of the arc of the flies, passage from bank to midstream is most likely to summon fish. On the one hand, no-brainer fishing; on the other, contemporary, intellectual technique and tackle.

Gene laughed every time he caught a fish. I could hear him over the rush of the current. "Aha!" he would say, like a cop on the beat back in the Bronx, having surprised a couple of teenagers spray-painting a mailbox. However, things turned out better for Bronx truants than they did for Gene's trout. A New York Italian American from the era of stickball and early doo-wop, Gene was constitutionally incapable of throwing back a trout. If he caught it, he ate it.

And, I must confess, so did I. It took a number of years for me to buy into catch-and-release trout fishing. It's not that I am opposed to killing them,

although I do think pressure can degrade a
fishery rather rapidly. I simply stopped
killing them for nearly twenty years.

But in those early days Gene and I killed
trout and drank Rob Roys (Gene's favorite
cocktail), and tied flies in between fishing
sessions. When I wasn't doing any of the
above, I practiced casting on the lawn.

Five happy years passed that way, fishing
with Gene. Then, one April morning, I
found myself in Grand Central on Opening
Day of trout season. Gene worked nearby at
J. Walter Thompson. What the hell, I thought,
we're not fishing so we might as well have a
highball at lunch (for those were the days
when even solid citizens still drank at lunch).

When I called his office the receptionist
asked, "Were you a friend of Gene's?"

I knew right then that Gene had died.
Heart attack. Forty-five years old, which is
way young, but I wasn't totally surprised.
He had told me once that his white hair was
the result of chemo ten years earlier. So all
that fishing, the way he looked at it, was on
borrowed time.

They buried him by the river at a cemetery
near a pool that we liked to fish. Often we
would have to trespass there to hit the river
at the right spot. A little trespassing never
bothered Gene, though. After all, he was
from the Bronx.

THE HEX OF THIRTEENTH LAKE

———◆———

I was a latecomer to the Adirondacks. It's a long drive from New York City, and in that same time on the road there are many other wonderful places that usually offer better fishing than the Adirondacks. That being said, once I started to fish there, like Winslow Homer and Teddy Roosevelt before me, I fell in love with its incomparable scenery. Add to that its great lore of fishing, canoeing, hiking, and climbing. Just being there makes me feel I have stepped—flannel shirt and all—into some 1930s fishing idyll that Ray Bergman might have written in *Field & Stream*. In short, the Adirondacks are still very much "blue highways" America: no malls, no Olive Gardens, no six-plex theaters—or at least as little of that as you are liable to find anywhere. So if the fishing isn't always blue ribbon, sometimes it is good, and in whatever way landscape talks to the soul, the Adirondacks talks to mine.

My introduction to the Adirondacks, like much else in my angling life, was a product of my friendship with Tom Akstens. He is the only Shakespeare Ph.D./Adirondacks guide/folksinger I know. Fishing with Tom is always a lot of laughs. He has the same healthy disrespect that I have for things in the mainstream. However, when it comes to fishing partners, the plain truth is that Tom Akstens and I are hexed. Though we are both reasonable anglers, there is no denying that over the course of thirty years and countless outings we have experienced a statistically improbable run of bad luck.

We have chased gulls, but not fish, around Buzzards Bay on Cape Cod during the peak of the striper run. We have paddled down the prodigiously bassy Grasse River in upstate New

York with few bass to show for it. In fact, I still half believe that it was our collectively lousy karma that brought on the floods of 1980 that devastated our beloved Esopus Creek.

But I am not talking about that kind of hex. I refer instead to *Hexagenia limbata*, a mayfly big as a silver dollar that hatches, among other places, in Adirondack lakes in July. Under the right conditions, it can bring trout to the surface, where they feed recklessly and voraciously.

"It's a lake version of the Green Drake," Tom told me, referring to its size and to the penchant of its nymphs for quiet water and burrowing in muck.

It is marvelous to fish this hatch wherever it takes place. I have caught beautiful trout at Hex time on the Fall River in northern California, and a few years later I took a lovely smallmouth on Dead Lake in the Upper Peninsula of Michigan.

So, when Akstens mentioned that he had heard of a Hex hatch on Lake Placid, it lodged in my memory as one of those things I needed to do one day. That day came a few years later. Tom had checked with a local fly shop owner who informed him that last year, at precisely the date we were thinking of fishing, the Hexes came out on Thirteenth Lake and the fishing had been great. "It was like bluefish off Long Island," was the optimistic report.

Acting on this hot tip, we loaded Akstens's red pickup truck and headed to Thirteenth Lake. From cross-country skiing, I knew Thirteenth as a splendid and isolated place. I imagined a fishing session in an Adirondack setting that a traveler in the nineteenth century described as "one of the nameless lakes that sleep in solitary beauty many miles

from any path or road, in the bosom of a natural forest, whose shades few travelers had entered."

Solitary wilderness? Not in the twenty-first century. At the boat launch, the parking lot was filled. Tents were pitched in every possible place near the shore. Stereos blared Led Zeppelin's greatest hits interspersed with some treacly Lee Greenwood and strident Eminem. Kids gave forth high-pitched

squeals as they ignored the chill in the air and the mosquitoes that had started to dive-bomb in earnest.

We loaded our canoe. The weight of a full knapsack, a trolling motor, and a heavy car battery made for quite a load, but Tom had a two-wheel canoe dolly and jury-rigged harness that allowed us to make our way fitfully along the path to the lake. I was reminded of the way Frank Sinatra and Sophia

Loren had schlepped their cannon around Spain in *The Pride and the Passion*.

Soon we were launched. The campground and its noise faded in the distance as we moved in the lee of a mountain. Just like that, we were alone except for a loon calling to one of his fellows across

the pond. Within a half hour we reached the end of the lake—which was where the Hexes would hatch . . . if they hatched.

Here and there the water stirred. Once or twice we thought we heard the splash of a feeding fish. Then a large mayfly appeared, popping open its wings like a waiter flapping open a linen napkin. The fly drifted,

as we did, with the wind. Then, gloriously, it disappeared with a slurp.

A Hex! Then, a few minutes later another one. Then, the rise forms of feeding trout. Tom rummaged through his fly boxes and produced an extended-body Green Drake that a friend had tied.

The next cast did the trick. The fly landed, sat there for a few seconds, and then disappeared into the mouth of a trout. Tom threw back hand cast at another rise form, and for the first time in our angling partnership, we had a double hookup.

The fish were not particularly big, but 12- and 13-inch trout on a light rod can be stimulating. And, anyway, the main kick is watching them take the fly, which you just happen to have on hand because you timed things right for the hatch. It feels like an affirmation of your righteousness as an angler.

For a half-hour we caught fish. Even in the dying light, the big flies were visible to the end.

With nothing left to prove, and no sign of big trout to keep us there, we decided to call it a night as the light left the sky. On the way back, three loons chorused. It sounded for all the world like laughter.

So we laughed.

DUNKED

—◆—

In my early fly-fishing days a man named Emil Grimm opened a fly shop in Phoenicia, New York. Emil was, pun intended, grim a lot of the time, partly because it was his nature but equally because the tubers had begun to chase out the fishermen on the Esopus. Tubers, so-called not because they had the brain of a potato, but because of the inner tubes in which they rode down the river. Often, sipping on a Bud, they would float between you and a rising fish. "How's it going?" they would ask. It got so that there were so many of them, if you got mad at each one of them you would have spent all your fishing time being pissed off. Whenever Tom Akstens and I stopped in at his shop, Emil would vent. Some time in July, he usually got fed up.

"Where are you going, Emil?" we asked.

"Up to the Ausable," he answered.

So for years, when I thought of the Ausable I thought of the rushing currents and big boulders that Emil described, and the tough wading, and the other curmudgeonly but dedicated anglers who were Emil's buddies. Then, one summer after Tom had moved up to the Adirondacks, my wife and I rented a great cabin. It was built in the early twentieth century: all twiggy, with lots of birch bark on the walls and rough-sawn planks for walls. It sat on the lower reaches of the West Branch of the Ausable. I could fish just outside my door, but instead I joined Tom on a bushwhack to a stretch known as the Bush Country.

Tom and his fellow guide, Rachel Finn, often called me in early June to let me know that they had just enjoyed amazing Green Drake fishing. Whole pools lit up with hundreds of trout. I always missed those mega-hatches. But still, I went with them to Bush Country whenever I had the chance. One night I accompanied Tom and Fritz Mitchell, another habitué of those rough-and-tumble waters.

When we arrived at the river, the air was wet from a passing rain. The understory of the forest was thick with aspen, wildflowers, and pale-green caribou moss. The leaves dripped with heavy summer mist and mosquitoes feasted on all warm-blooded creatures. In the late sun, the Tinker Bell flutter of insect wings filled the air with sparkling light. Large gray *Isonychia* hatched in numbers. Even larger *Isonychia* spinners dipped to the surface. Because of their long white-tipped legs, they are vernacularly known as White Gloved Howdies. Yes, it was the same fly that Gino Calogero referred to when I first met him on the Esopus, but it was only on this trip, thirty years later, that Fritz informed me that the fly was called by this name after the practice of old-time politicians who wore white gloves on their glad-handing forays.

The water was high. The wading was a bear. Fritz, who prefers to fish rough pocket water, spotted the broad shoulders of a rising fish. He directed me to the best place to cast across the complex current. I leaned on my wading staff and fought my way out. I cast. The fish rose. My fly dragged. The fish went down. I presented my fly again. He rose again but, on subsequent casts, neglected to reappear.

"Funny thing, Fritz," I said. "My experience on pocket water is that the fish are opportunistic and not too picky. They should keep rising to the fly."

"They will rise at first," he explained. "But I find that you get one or two shots and if they don't take, move on."

With that he suggested we made to the next good trout lie upstream. I turned in the current and inched my way toward shore. The river nudged me downstream. When I lifted my foot, it was like stepping off a ledge. I experienced the disquieting—oh damn!—inevitability to that split second between the moment you know you have stepped too far into a swift current and the moment it overflows your waders. You have a clear sense of having reached the tipping point, a feeling of the world slowing down as it does before a traffic crash. There's nothing you can do about it except get wet. The water lapped over the top of my waders. Cold wetness filled my boots. I recoiled from the shock and pressed on to the bank.

"At least you weren't swept downstream," Akstens consoled.

Wet, but determined to get even with the trout, I joined my comrades for the march upstream. We forded at a non-suicidal spot and entered the water below the outlet of a feeder creek. I waded ever so gingerly into the flat water where I expected to see risers to the *Isonychia*. There were none.

Fritz strode into the pocket water with the ease of a bison walking through tall grass. He tied on a Gray Wulff and—bam, bam, bam, bam—took four nice brook trout. He advised me to cast near some rocks and to pass by others. Every rock that he thought would yield a trout, did: all lovely brookies.

"If you are up for it," he suggested, "the flat rock below the pool takes some wading, but I know there's a nice fish there."

"No way," I said wimpishly.

"You're doing it," he commanded.

I fought through the current, bird-dogging Fritz's footsteps. He found a spot where there was enough gravel to dig your feet in. He gave me a Stimulator, a good pocket-water pattern that imitates a large stonefly. Per his instructions, I laid out a long cast and threw an upstream mend when it hit the water. The fly floated through a slick and then past the trunk of a deadfall against the far bank.

Nothing.

I cast again. The fly spun in the eddy. Just at the point where drag was about to set in, a large, fat rainbow slammed it, and in the same motion, rocketed a foot into the air.

Tom whooped with excitement. Fritz too. He counseled me to edge my way backward to the bank and then to fight the fish as I followed it downstream. I declined: I would beat the fish where I stood or I would lose him, but I wasn't going to take another dunking.

The rainbow proved pugnacious but compliant. Within minutes I had him in my hands. He was the best fish and certainly the most dramatic one of my trip. Being cold and wet was, at that moment, very beside the point.

HOLY WATER: The Delaware

———◆———

*I*neffable natural beauty is inexplicable. *The Delaware River is one such place. Oddly, the site of my first mystical communion with the river is a spot that I have never fished. It is the swirly, jade-colored water at the confluence of the Lackawaxen and the Delaware. Zane Gray, who in addition to his wonderful fictional pieces wrote great fishing prose, spent nearly ten years there as a postmaster. Clearly it inspired him.

Facing upstream, you see the Lackawaxen as it feeds in from the left while the full force of the main stem of the river pushes down on it. The result is a bottom strewn with large boulders, a bend in the river to the right, and in that hook every possible kind of current and eddy. The green water and the constant play of light can only be described as psychedelic. Stare at it and you might soon think you are looking at a rose window in a medieval cathedral as it catches the full light of the sun. Stare even more deeply and you might even see, as I did, the silver flash of a hundred shad coursing upstream.

I first heard about the Delaware as a trout-fishing destination about two years after I took up the fly rod on the Esopus. It was early in the morning, and I had decided to walk through the woods to a famous hot spot known as the Chimney Hole. The car parked in front of mine was a light-tan van whose driver had opened the back door, reached in, and pulled out the biggest brown trout I had ever seen.

"How big?" I asked.

"Eleven pounds."

"Where did you get it?"

"On the Delaware."

I filed the info as Duly Noted, but it took about ten years before I actually made it to the Delaware. I kept fishing the Esopus and, when it was off, I traveled to the Schoharie, or other streams within a half hour's drive. But over the years, the Esopus fishery petered out, the Schoharie silted in, and the Beaverkill, which was far, but not as far as the Delaware, ran hot in high summer.

Once I started to fish the Delaware, though, it became the only trout stream in the Catskills. The Delaware system includes the main stem of the river as well as the east and west branches. It is, in my mind, the jewel in the crown of East Coast trout streams, especially during June, July, and August, when cold-water bottom releases from the Cannonsville and Pepacton Reservoirs create a dependable tailwater fishery with big wild trout that feed on prolific and equally dependable mayfly hatches. If the state, which controls the level of these reservoirs, would ensure the regularity of flow, the Delaware would be mentioned in the same breath as other fabled tailwaters such as Montana's Missouri or the White River in Arkansas.

My first forays were on the East Branch, which was exactly 52 miles from my brother's house in Woodstock. It was a long way to drive, but in summer a hatch of Sulphurs could be counted on at 3:30 in the afternoon. At that hour the fish would take up their stations in pods of six or eight. As the exquisite mayflies floated down the current lines in long flotillas, fat brown trout rose rhythmically . . . mesmerizingly.

My fishing partner on most of those early trips to the East Branch in the late 1970s was Ben Montanelli, who is one of the fortunate fraternity that flat-out knows how to catch fish. There was nothing about his cast—which is good but not amazing—that made me think that he was something special. But never judge an angler by the cast. I can cast pretty far for someone who doesn't make his living at it, but I can't catch fish the way Ben can. He has that special ability to think about what the fly is doing at the end of his cast. Most of us decide where we want to put the fly and feel that once it has been delivered, we have taken our shot and the rest is up to the fish. Ben, on the other hand, is one of those rare anglers who pictures the fly in the water as the fish will see it and then puts his cast together, thinking from the water back to the rod.

When the Sulphurs hatched, more often than not, I put down every fish I cast to. The one exception was when, after careful wading, I got off a good cast to the lead fish in the pod. After that, the commotion sent the rest of the trout packing. Ben, though, would work his way up from the back of the school to the head, always positioning himself so that the leader covered, at most, one fish. Delaware River trout are wild, wily, selective, and—when you catch, or even hook, one—satisfying.

From those first experiences on the East Branch, I moved on to the main stem and the West Branch. I have Tom Colicchio to thank for that. I was working with Colicchio, the chef of Craft and Gramercy Tavern in New York, for a cover story for *New York Magazine*. Although the piece was about the opening of Gramercy, when I discovered that Tom was a fly-

rodder, I knew that I had found a way to spend quality time with him, the kind of time that gives depth to a story. And, oh yeah, we got to fish too.

Through Tom, I was introduced to the West Branch, which has the same cold water and wild fish as the East Branch, but with even more of a classic, riffle-pool configuration. On our first trip there I

had intended to do a story about gathering ramps (kind of a strong white onion) and morels. Tom would cook a streamside meal. Even if we had not been catch-and-release anglers, a perfect spring meal of trout, ramps, and morels was not in the cards. The plain facts of the matter are that Delaware fish taste like mud. Good for the fish, good for the fishing, bad for the menu.

Colicchio made up for it with a boneless veal roast that he planned to cook over the campfire. That idea, however, went partially off the tracks because of a midday rainstorm that soaked our firewood. No matter: Colicchio got out his little Coleman stove and proceeded to demonstrate what makes a good chef. With nothing but that stove, and equally rinky-dink pots and pans, he made a stew of ramps and morels and pan-roasted the veal, gauging its degree of doneness with a wonderful trick that I have since employed many times.

Hold out one hand, palm up, fingers together. With the index finger of your free hand jab the fleshy part of your other hand—right above the thumb and below the index finger.

"That's how raw meat

feels," Colicchio advised.

Now take that same hand—the one with the fingers together—and spread your fingers. Jab the same part just above the thumb. "That's cooked," Colicchio continued.

In this manner he poked and prodded the veal roast until it felt just right.

Colicchio introduced me to Al Caucci, one of the legends of modern fly-fishing who has since become a fishing partner and friend on the Delaware, out at Montauk, and down in the Keys. Caucci's invention (with Bob Nastasi) of the Comparadun fly, more than any other advance, made it more feasible to fish highly selective trout on technical water. For a dry-fly angler, this is the peak of the game.

As I think about this splendid river, it strikes me that my relationship with the Delaware has been about my friendship with Italian Americans. Like all Italians I have ever known, Ben, Tom, and Al are fond of good food.

This is a fortunate thing. Despite the fact that trout are beautiful, rivers are beautiful, and good trout fishing only happens in pretty places, it is also true that the food in most trout-fishing meccas is not so great. Caucci, whose family comes from Ascoli Piceno in Le Marche, was so upset about the lack of good food on the Delaware that he hired a real Italian chef, Fabio Chindemo, to cook at his lodge during the high season.

A five- or six-course meal, good wine, and equally good talk are an unbeatable way to end a fishing day. In failure, it will console you, and in success it will add to your happiness, never more so

than it did mine one cool and foggy night in June.

My daughter Lucy, after her first year in college, was planning a cross-country drive. Only one obstacle stood in her way—a driver's license. She had already failed her road test. This did not displease me as her tentative departure date approached. Lucy was determined, though, and through a lot of Internet searching was able to schedule an appointment on short notice in Delhi, New York.

It was about a four-hour drive from our home, and I suppose I could have argued her out of it on the grounds of not being able to blow a whole day in the car. On the other hand, Delhi is about forty-five minutes from Caucci's, and the Green Drake spinner fall was set to happen any time.

"Okay," I told Lucy, "if it means that much to

you, let's do it. And as long as we are there we can go over to Al's after the test. We'll fish and have dinner and stay the night."

So I gave the wheel to Lucy and she drove us upstate. She did well, but I think her nerves got to her because she was a little aggressive on her road test and the inspector flunked her. Lucy was big-time depressed. The weather, cold and damp, fit her mood as we hit the river with Wiley Paul, one of Al's extremely obliging and well-trained guides.

The river looked dead, but Paul was not discouraged. "I know of a few steady feeders," he promised, and within ten minutes we saw the regular rise of a big fish that held tight to the bank. Just in front of it a clump of earth partially diverted the current. It required a demanding left reach cast. I thought that Lucy did not have the casting skills nor the trout sense to put the fly where it needed to be. And had the fish taken it, I was sure she would be too hard on the hookset and break off.

I was wrong. For an hour and a half she worked the fish, changing flies, changing drifts, changing angles, and she never put it down. Still, I thought the fish was uncatchable. Again, I was wrong. Lucy cast. We all stared at her fly slowly advancing with the current. It rode a tiny eddy into the trout's window and, ever so subtly, the trout sucked it in. Lucy came tight, and the fight was joined. At this juncture, had it been the two of us, my excitement would have got the better of me and for sure I would have barked confusing orders. But Paul kept his cool and talked Lucy through the fight. When it was over she cradled a 19 ½-inch brown trout with a gorgeous kype. For the record, I have never taken anything over 16

inches in thirty years of fishing the Catskills.

The fact that the Coffin flies, as the Green Drake spinners are called, were blown out by a sundown wind, just as they were about to hit the water, could not dampen our spirits. For that matter neither could the rain that followed. Back at Caucci's, Lucy was the only female at a table of voluble, middle-aged trout fishermen. Sipping her wine, she joined in the conversation quite easily and exercised her considerable talent as a storyteller as she recounted her conquest.

It would be hard to find anything that could gladden a father's heart much more.

P.S. She got her license the next week and drove to California.

LORDS OF THE FLY:
The Babe Ruth of Fishing

———◆———

If you were asked to name one, and only one, great baseball player, chances are you would say Babe Ruth.
No one would call you nuts if you had mentioned Joe DiMaggio or Ty Cobb, but for excellence, no less than fame, the Babe is Mr. Baseball. In American fly fishing the same could be said of Lee Wulff. Had he not lent his name to the Wulff series of flies, we would still celebrate him as the inventor of the fishing vest. And had he done neither of these things, his angling prowess would nonetheless have established his place in fly-fishing's pantheon.

But Lee Wulff did all of the above. Add in matinee-idol good looks and a clipped, sure vocal delivery that was a cross between Gary Cooper's and Clint Eastwood's, and he couldn't have been anything but a star.

He is most famous for his invention of the Wulff series of hairwing flies. When all else fails, what fisherman hasn't said, "What the hell, I'll tie on a Royal Wulff"? Like a prayer sent to heaven by a desperate man, the gaudy fly does the trick . . . some of the time.

"In the winter of '29–'30," he told me when I first visited him in 1982, "I got to thinking about flies. It seemed that the classic eastern patterns were often too delicate, too slim. The only fly we had with some body to it and some visibility in rough water was the Fan Wing Royal Coachman, but that was a very fragile fly. For some reason I thought of using bucktail instead of feathers, so I tied a grey hairwing to imitate the Gray Drake of the Ausable or the Dark Hendrickson of the Catskill streams. I also tied a white one to imitate the Coffin fly.

"I tried the Grey Wulff first, on the Esopus Creek, and caught fifty fish with it before it ceased to produce. Dan Bailey was with me that day and he really liked the new flies. Bailey designed the rest of the Wulff series, and it was Dan who named the flies after me. The Wulffs were the only bucktail dry flies in the 1932 edition of Ray Bergman's *Trout*, and I think that was the key to their catching on so well."

Another Wulff invention of the 1930s was the fishing vest. "A vest was something you wore under clothes. I thought why not put it outside, sew a lot of pockets on it, and end up with a way to keep your tackle organized and dry. I sewed that first vest myself out of denim that I bought at Macy's."

As he spoke, he fashioned a fluffy Grey Wulff, then an impossibly small size 28 variant. Even for the youngest, sharpest eyes and the most dexterous fingers that is no small feat. Wulff did it without a vise!

Wulff was born in Alaska, and first fished there, but left in his early adolescence when the family moved to Brooklyn, New York, where he attended Erasmus Hall High School. After college, he went to Paris, where he was set on becoming an artist. After a year of bohemian life, he returned to New York and landed at Dupont, designing packages.

Work was hard to come by in those Depression years, and most men would have been grateful for any job, but Lee Wulff was restive. "I was making $35 a week at Dupont until they cut me back to $31.50. There was nothing much to be done about it, though, because there were people standing in line for your job. I really got fed up when they fired an old guy who was just two months short of his pension. I decided right then and there that competing for money was foreign to me. I'd write, draw, lecture, and do whatever I had to do to buy my time back. I took the summer off. I did some freelancing. I camped on the Beaverkill where a campsite ran me $3.50 a week."

Unemployed, but unencumbered, Wulff was free to devote his time to the outdoors. It would be a fertile period. In 1937, he entered the first International Tuna Tournament in Nova Scotia. Of the five fish that were caught during the contest, Wulff took two, including a 560-pounder. This last earned a photograph in the *New York Times*. An official of the Newfoundland government noted Wulff's picture and invited him to explore the possibilities of opening the province to sport fishing.

Just think of it: thousands of square miles of virgin waters brimming with brook trout, rivers full of Atlantic salmon, swordfish and tuna cruising offshore, and caribou moving along forest trails that had never felt the impress of a boot or moccasin.

I spent the better part of a week watching the movies that Lee made in Canada in the late 1930s and continued on through his work of the 1960s and 1970s when he hosted the first network outdoors shows. As I sat alone in the darkened room, his name filled the screen, a tidy signature that reminded me of Walt Disney's logo. The music was typical 1930s newsreel music that could have underscored a scene of bathing beauties playing water polo. In the very first shot, the screen was filled with color: color in 1938! I had always thought that *The Wizard of Oz* was the first color movie, but Lee said that Kodak had given him some film to test a year earlier.

42

The first film opened on young Wulff, tall and lean with a shock of wavy brown hair and a flannel shirt, a guileless American frontiersman. He canoes up a stream. The sun throws the angler into high contrast. In the foreground, his line uncoils like a bullwhip. A streamer fly follows, darting through the current. A 5-pound brookie strikes and comes to net. The scene changes to the high seas, and Wulff hooks into a bluefin. The crew backs the boat down as the fish runs. Much later the blue giant surrenders to the gaff and is lashed aboard. The crew hoists a white flag emblazoned with a black tuna, an angler's Jolly Roger.

The scene shifts again, and Lee catches a sea run brookie in the surf. Then, on another river, he hooks a salmon, plays it, and lands it with yet another of his inventions, the tailer, a mechanical noose that locks around the salmon's tail, allowing for a quick and harmless release. Finally a hauntingly beautiful sequence of hundreds of salmon, leaping but not clearing a raging waterfall. The foam piles high as the silver torpedoes hurl themselves skyward, again and again, only to fall back. The scene has the grainy, out-of-focus look of a dream half remembered.

As the film ended, Lee flicked on the lights, and in response to my questions, he began to philosophize on the outdoors. Among the gems, and there were many, two have stayed with me.

"To fish you must think like a predator. The predator is always stronger than his prey. He can out-hink it, outrun it, overpower it. The hawk can outfly the dove. How, then, does the dove survive? He can outreproduce his pursuers. He survives on love.

"When you fish for salmon you fish for his memory, the memories of his early life in the stream when flies made up his diet. Even though he no longer eats them, in fact doesn't eat at all on his spawning run, he will sometimes strike the fly—a jolt from memory. With other fish, you fish for their hunger, but not the salmon. It is the memory."

Over the next few years Lee and I stayed in touch, talking on the phone, having a meal up at the old Antrim Lodge in Roscoe, New York, hunting for grouse and woodcock on the mountainsides outside of Margaretville. He flew me around the Catskills in his small plane, following the courses of the Beaverkill, the Delaware, the Esopus. Like me, he could not help from trying to pick out rise forms from 3,000 feet in the air.

After one such flight the Beaverkill looked so good that we simply had to fish it. I didn't have any flies, so Lee lent me a box that he had tied. Interestingly they were all tied variant style. All hackle, no wings—not very orthodox but a style that I, too, preferred. The pool may have looked good but it was dead. I put down my rod, picked up a stone, and skipped it across the river. Lee came over and did the same. We were just like two kids killing time.

BONEY FISH ON THE DELAWARE

———————◆———————

The shad, though it may not have the aristocratic lore of the trout, nor the roustabout reputation of the largemouth and smallmouth bass, has one thing going for it that neither the true trout nor the basses have: the shad comes from here. By here I mean my part of the country, the Northeast. Long before Columbus, or even Leif Ericsson, American shad ascended the rivers between Connecticut and the Carolinas. The trout, in contrast, did not make his appearance until the latter half of the nineteenth century, and the freshwater basses waited until the century was nearly done.

Maybe the shad doesn't get a lot of respect because he is just a large herring. But, then, so is the lordly tarpon, and he occupies a lofty rung on the fly-fishing ladder. I think part of the reason the shad never achieved high status is that he is boney. Also, he is only here for a couple of weeks each year. But it is always a glorious time of year, between the first dogwoods and the last cherry blossoms. Moreover he—actually make that she—provides New York with a homegrown delicacy as toothsome as the truffles of Perigord or the hams of Extremadura. I refer, of course, to shad roe, once a mainstay of springtime menus back in the gilded days when Goulds and Astors, Roosevelts and Rockefellers, dined at Delmonico's.

Which is a long way of saying, I like shad. I first fished for them on the Lower Delaware, below Dingmans Ferry. My college roommate, Ed Broderick, had fished at his family's little camp on the river ever since World War II, when the owners of the old Dutch Land Grant had allowed a bunch of vets to park their campers and old buses down by the river. Over time a little community grew up that came to life for a few weeks each year when the shad run was on. I called the little community Shadtown and returned to it often.

The residents of Shadtown had a marvelous solution to the boniness problem. If you caught a couple of shad, you gave them to one of the locals who kept a smoker going. In return for your brace of fresh shad, he gave you back a single smoked shad. I loved to eat these fish for lunch on the first hot days of the year. With cold beer, watercress salad, and freshly made dill mayonnaise, it was the best!

Some years later, when I had branched out into food writing, one of the most enjoyable stories for me to research involved my taking 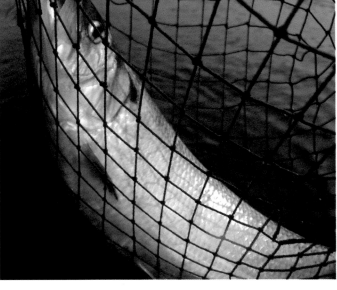 two of New York's top chefs up to Al Caucci's on the Delaware. Our assignment: to make a gourmet meal out of food that we picked or caught. Chamomile Sherbet and Wild Strawberry Compote, American Eel with Cattail Hearts. And, for the shad course, Gray Kunz, who was then the chef of America's top-rated Lespinasse, sautéed up a pair of shad roe

with wild ramps and homemade maple syrup along with vinegar made from that syrup. True to the form I have seen established over the years, I received more letters about that single story than five years worth of pure fishing or pure food stories. There's something about catching and cooking that captivates readers.

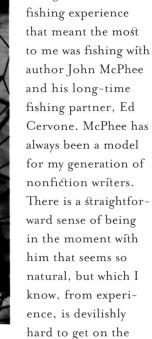

As an angler, though, the shad-fishing experience that meant the most to me was fishing with author John McPhee and his long-time fishing partner, Ed Cervone. McPhee has always been a model for my generation of nonfiction writers. There is a straightforward sense of being in the moment with him that seems so natural, but which I know, from experience, is devilishly hard to get on the page. He loves to fish for shad with a fly rod. His book *The Founding Fish* is a marvelous example how, by looking at one thing deeply enough, you may learn about many things.

I first fished with John on a warm May afternoon. We met at the boat ramp in Lambertville, New Jersey, where he greeted me with a swordsman-like flourish

of his fly rod. Ed Cervone arrived soon after, trailering his boat. Within minutes we were on the water, making our way upstream. Like two men analyzing the lay of a pool table, the fishing partners discussed where we would anchor. Proper placement is ninety percent of the game. Shad, they explained, seek a strong current, following it like a trail to their spawning grounds. They are very precise about how they respond to this factor. You may be just upstream of someone catching fish after fish, but if you have not accounted for a submerged ledge, a small eddy, a slight shift of current, then you will spend your afternoon watching someone else's good time. As McPhee has written: "While personally spending nine hundred and twenty-two hours on or in the river in many different places fishing for shad, I have developed a distinct impression that a hundred thousand people have crowded ahead of me into positions superior to mine."

Sure enough, precisely at that point where Ed intended to drop anchor, an angler of tremendous girth in a boat brandishing four rods had taken up position and, by the bend of his pole, appeared to be fighting a fish.

We anchored just upcurrent of him. At first we were heartened by his luck but as he succeeded and we were stalemated, our comments went from admiring to envious to unprintable.

Finally Ed's rod dipped as he fought a strong male, or buck, as aficionados say. The fight was long but eventually ended in favor of the angler. The buck went into the cooler and we returned to our positions. Waiting, waiting, waiting, while the man in front of us continued his relentless harvest. John suggested,

understandably, that we hang him, although he may have meant this as a figure of speech.

Ed, who is a very observant angler, said, "That guy is just letting his line hang in the current, not moving it at all. Why don't we do that?"

I did as instructed. I suppose you might say this is not really fly-fishing, but rather, using a fly-rod to leave your shad dart, as the traditional lure is called, to dance in the current seam.

"Now drop the tip so that you are fishing on the bottom of the river."

Wondrously, no sooner had I dipped my rod then my line went taut and there commenced a satisfying tussle with a beautiful roe shad. It took a good ten minutes to ease her to the net. When we laid her on the deck her scales shone silver with a wash of pinkish magenta.

We returned to Ed's home in Pennington and scaled the fish on some newspapers that we spread on the lawn. We delivered the cleaned shad to Ed's wife, Marian, who removed the flesh from the bones. Marian set about preparing a slow-cooked recipe that her mom first saw on a t.v. show in the 1950s on which the chef from the Waldorf Astoria appeared. I marveled at the amount of prep work involved. It has been my experience that labor-intensive recipes that one learns from one's mother are often an ancient family tradition. That Marian's mom would have just up and done it after watching a t.v. show and that Marian would have continued the tradition, I take as the hallmarks of true food lovers. I now make it once each year as my slow-food rite of spring.

Serves 4

Shad Roast

	Heat oven to 350°F.
2 boned fillets from	Lay first fillet skin-side down in
a 4-6 pound roe shad	a Dutch oven or lasagna pan and season with salt and pepper.
(Do yourself a favor and have	Cover with roe sacs and season again.
the fish store do it.)	Lay 3 strips of bacon, lengthwise, on roe.
Salt and pepper to taste	Place second fillet, skin-side up, over bacon.
1 pair shad roe sacs	Lay remaining 3 strips of bacon lengthwise on skin of second filet.
6 strips bacon	Pour wine into pan. Cover and place in oven for 1¼ hours.
½ cup white wine	Remove cover and place pan under broiler until bacon is crisp.
Lemon wedges	Slice shad as you would a meatloaf and serve with lemon wedges.

A LITTLE STREAM

———◆———

Little streams are rarely crowded. There is a trout every place you would expect to find one: in every deep hole, at the edge of every current line, behind every rock, under every overhanging bough, tucked into every shadowy undercut bank. A well-presented fly should raise a fish. If it doesn't summon a trout—at least for a look—you have not cast well. All anglers have a little stream, and at some point they learn that most big streams can be fished as if they were a collection of little streams. My little stream flowed in to the Esopus. It came from Shady, down through Willow, to Mt. Tremper.

I went there when I felt like fishing and not making a big deal out of it. For instance, there was the Fourth of July when my younger brother, Donald, and I stole away from the family's pre-barbecue preparations for a few hours' fishing. We were on Guardian Mountain in the town of Shady, just outside of Woodstock, New York. We toyed with the idea of driving over to the East Branch of the Delaware, but quickly settled on the nearby feeder that ran to the Esopus. We'd gain an hour's fishing time, we reasoned.

We prospected, driving up and down Route 212, pulling over wherever the creek came near the road. We noted its architecture, the way this year's rains had moved things around. We parked by a nice run. The day was warm, so we left our waders in the car. Not having to put on waders is one of the great joys of summer fishing, especially on little creeks where, for the most part, you are hopping from boulder to boulder or along the bank.

I walked downstream. Don went up. Soon, Donald was fast to a fish. He brought it to hand, bent down, and released it.

I cast an Ausable Wulff into the current. A fish rose and refused it. You will often provoke a rise on your first cast on these little creeks, and you will see the whole rise as the fish comes out from under a rock and ascends through the water. If you get a refusal, continue on. You will only get one rise per fish.

I got out of the stream and walked to the tail of a little pool before changing flies. I entered below the pool, standing behind a rock at the head of the next pool. I was well concealed and my movements would not disturb the current above me. I think of this manner of fishing as "stepping stone" fishing, with the steps being a series of little pools that mark the descent of the river course.

A small mayfly hatch was coming off: a bright yellow body and purple wings. I tied on a Pale Evening Dun. Its ginger hackle had the shimmering aspect of the classic sparsely tied Catskill dry fly. A brown trout splashed. I laid the cast into his feeding lane. He took. I struck. Ten inches and fat.

As I write this I think of the especially delicious times on this creek, on hot afternoons when it was too early or too much of a pain to fish in the main stem of the Esopus. I'd clamber down the bank from my cabin wearing cutoffs and sneakers, carrying three

or four flies and one roll of tippet. I'd cast my way up the stepping stones for a half mile or so. Sometimes deer would come down to drink, or a grouse would flush from behind a hollow log. Once I spent a half hour watching a snake trying to swallow a trout. The serpent had clamped down on the

trout crosswise, but it could only swallow it by maneuvering so that the fish went in tail first.

This little stream had just about every kind of trout water. There were pools up to forty feet long so the trout could distribute themselves just like the diagrams in fishing books. There were little waterfalls and, in the heat of the summer, eager trout in the heavily aerated water below each cataract. There was one long flat stretch where I had cast a thousand times to a pair of beautiful brown trout, the very biggest browns in the stream (it was mostly rainbow water).

For many years I had come to this spot at the end of the day and tried for the browns. Reach casts, pile casts, dapping casts, but the nature of the currents, the configuration of berry bushes and trees, and the height of the bank limited the possible presentations. What was really needed was a hatch to move the fish out from the bank, and in such water, there were few hatches.

It was maddening. You could see the fish finning in five feet of water so clear that it might have been air. I would kneel, which was the only way a back cast could find its way through the spreading boughs of a dead apple tree.

For a couple of seasons a red-winged blackbird made her nest in the old tree. When her hatchlings were in the nest I had to be super quiet because as soon as they stirred, Mom returned and raised holy hell. This alarm made the skittish trout impossibly wary. Shamefully, on a few occasions, rather than laying down my rod, I kept casting and the mother red-wing kept circling more furiously. It was my hope that I could get her so worked up that she would keel over from a heart attack. That strategy never panned out.

That afternoon with my brother stands out perhaps because we so rarely had the chance to fish together because of his heavy work schedule as a doctor and his equally heavy weekend schedule as the father of three sports-obsessed sons. I can still see a nice fish that rose regularly under the satiny

lip of a little waterfall. Don tied a small Adams to a very long leader and sailed it into the edge of the upwelling of the water. It settled for an instant, rotated a quarter turn, and then the fish hit. A rainbow: 14–15 inches, quite large for that stream. On the first leap he flew out of the shadow of the waterfall into the sunlight. He was deep blue on the sides, shot through with gold in the belly. He broke off after another jump.

"Nice," I said.

"Goddammit," Don replied.

We continued to fish, hitting all the likely spots, raising a number of trout, catching a few. We caught a dozen between us. None of them were big, but they were fun, and we retired from the stream contented.

Though we didn't catch anything of size that afternoon, there are big fish in the stream. In the spring, I have seen people take spawning rainbows up to 24 inches. And while grouse hunting in the fall, I have come across spawning brown trout that were as large as the rainbows.

The trophy fish of that year had been caught by a non-angler at the end of June, long after the spawning run. A tourist was sunning herself by the riverbank when she noticed a commotion in the stream. She saw a large trout trying to buck its way up current. It hit a rock and lay stunned. The curious lady lifted the dazed trout out by hand and brought it to the kitchen of La Duchesse Anne, a lovely streamside French restaurant and my longtime watering hole. The chef reported that it weighed four pounds and was, in addition, quite delicious.

PAN-ROASTED FISH
with Aromatic Salted Herbs

—◆—

I *have only fly-fished for salmon once in America, for raggedy, old, spawned-out fish on the Salmon River in* upstate New York. They looked like they had shown up at a casting call for the salmon version of *The Mummy's Revenge*. You may fish for Pacific salmon all over the Great Lakes and in their home range on the Pacific Coast. I did have the pleasure, once, of fishing for Atlantic Salmon in the Pana River in Russia. The way our guides prepared them there was to make a fire, let the coals burn down, then cover the fish with butter, slivered garlic, dill, salt, and pepper. They sealed the wrapping and placed the fish on the embers. The first day we tried it, the fish was quite dry.

The only thing less expert than the guide's English was my Russian, but finally, by pointing at my watch and making a series of signs, I was able to communicate that I was asking how long they had cooked the fish.

"Twenty minutes," they indicated.

"Bake it for ten," I signed back.

The next day they followed my suggestion. No go, still dry. I had them cut the time to five minutes. Same result.

I think there's something about Russian salmon, or maybe Russian fires, that makes for dry fish.

The following recipe, however, is never dry. It was invented by Gray Kunz, a brilliant chef with whom I wrote the book *The Elements of Taste*. We wanted something fresh-tasting with lots of herbs and salt. Gray's solution was to cook the fish so that it was done on the outside and just at the point of flakiness inside.

I have tried this with striper and tuna, both of which you can catch on the fly, and cod, which in my experience is not a fly-rod fish. You might want to start with salmon, however.

Serves 4

Herbs

2 tablespoons chopped fresh chives
½ cup loosely packed chopped fresh flat-leaf parsley
⅓ cup loosely packed chopped fresh mint
⅓ cup chopped fresh dill

Combine all the herbs in a small bowl and set aside.

Salt and Spice Mix

1½ tablespoons kosher salt
⅛ teaspoon cayenne pepper
⅛ teaspoon ground cardamom
½ teaspoon ground nutmeg
½ teaspoon coarsely ground white pepper

Combine all the ingredients for the salt and spice mix in another small bowl and set aside.

Salmon

1½ pounds salmon fillet, cut into 4 servings
2 tablespoons peanut oil
2 tablespoons unsalted butter
Kosher salt
Cayenne pepper

Preheat the oven to 225°F.

Heat the oil in a large ovenproof skillet over medium-high heat. Add the salmon skin-side down and cook until crisp, about 2 minutes. Season the salmon with salt and cayenne to taste. Dot the salmon with the butter, place in the oven, and bake 4 to 6 minutes, or until flaky.

Arrange the fillets on warm plates, then sprinkle with the herbs. Dust lightly with the salt and spice mix, and serve.

THE WEST

A Yellowstone Honeymoon

No matter how well you have come to know it, Yellowstone Park retains an aura of primal mystery. Even in August, when RVs and campers, tourists, and caterwauling toddlers overfill the campgrounds and back up traffic for the most minor wildlife sighting, you still know that when you gaze at the geysers and fumaroles and the wide pale-green valleys, you are looking at the blood and bones of the earth.

If you have a naturalist streak in you that all fly fishermen are thought to share, it is contemplation of such vistas that supposedly awakens a higher morality in the angler's soul—at least that is how generations of writers have seen it, spurred, no doubt, in part by a desire to justify the frittering away of hours waving a stick at a river.

I evinced none of the standard awestruck wonder of the nature lover on my first visit to Yellowstone Park. My guide was Larry Aiuppy, the bear-sized and highly intellectual photographer and fly fisherman of Livingston, Montana.

"There's the Mammoth Terraces," he said, nodding his head to indicate the white limestone cascade that tumbled and steamed down the mountainside—the petrified stop-motion flow of volcanically heated water.

"Yeah, sure. Keep driving," I said, with more impatience at getting to the stream than awe at nature's handiwork.

A half hour later we arrived at Slough Creek. Okay, now I was ready to receive the wonder. The wide bowl of the valley surrounded me, the hills carpeted in grass whose green was the pastel shade that you see on the underside of new leaves in the spring. The creek lay below us, a rather short walk. There were two other anglers in view, a far cry from the crowds that I had been told populated the lower stretch. Common wisdom was that you had to hike a mile or two upstream to hope to find the beginning of good fishing. But sometimes it pays to buck the tide of common opinion.

Instead of trudging upstream, we had a short walk across a field that leads to the gorgeous meander of Slough Creek. As happens often on streams in the Yellowstone drainage, the indigenous cutthroat cohabited with the more common rainbow that has supplanted the cutts in much of their original range.

Aiuppy explained the fish geography of a typical pool: how rainbows would hang on the swifter part of the current seam and cutthroats on the sinuous bubble line where the water still moved but with less force and velocity.

That I missed five big rainbows tells you something about the quality of fish in Slough Creek in those days but just as much about the quality of my angling. At that stage, I had not yet caught enough big trout (by big I mean a fish that will take line off the reel). As Aiuppy talked me through it, I learned such fish must be struck and played with some finesse.

My wife, Melinda, was a case of love at first bite. And speaking of love, Melinda and I returned to Slough on our honeymoon, where, through trout greediness, I incurred a big karmic debt, whose secret I have kept locked up inside me for years, not telling a soul . . . until now.

On our first trip into the park, Melinda and I combined admiring the scenery with a fishing session at Buffalo Ford on the Yellowstone. This is one of those witching waters that I hold dear in the same part of my heart reserved for the Zane Gray stretch of the Delaware, the tarpon reef off of Elliot Key's Florida, the mouth of the Chimehuin in Patagonia, and Caswell's Point near Montauk.

The Yellowstone, through all of its flow, has a steep gradient, with the result that even in shallow spots it pushes against you with great force. To reach a particularly fishy-looking braid in the river, we had to wade a channel near the base of an island.

I buffaloed my way across stream, on fire with an angling lust that had been kindled by a pool full of rises and the air above it aflutter with PMDs.

Melinda called for me.

I turned to see my forlorn newlywed, her clothes dripping wet.

"The current knocked me over," she said sadly.

"And as I fell I let go of the rod and it floated downstream."

I gulped. That was my Orvis trout rod, a 6 weight that had caught trout, Everglades largemouth, Keys bones, Labrador brook trout. It was my go-to fishing tool.

"No big deal," I lied. "I have an extra rod."

A few days later, we went to Slough Creek with Janny Aiuppy, Larry's wife and a fine angler. We returned to the very spot where Larry and I had first fished a few years before. I dropped down the pool to some flat water with undercut banks and big fish.

Using one of my favorite flies, the incredibly buggy-looking Griffith's Gnat, I managed to entice a 26-inch cutthroat to the fly. What a fish! The biggest trout I ever caught until I took on the sea-run browns

of Tierra del Fuego. The fish ate the fly with the spectacular head-and-tail take of the cutthroat. In contrast to a rainbow or brown, who takes and either disappears or leaps skyward, the cutthroat comes up to eat, followed by the whole length of his body, before diving back down to fight.

Somehow I landed that fish, which to this day remains the biggest cutthroat I have ever hooked, let alone landed. It was my good fortune that I had him in a pool with no deadfalls or other obstructions.

I released him and Melinda joined me for a look at some of the water downstream. We walked quietly along the banks so that our footfalls did not reverberate like kettle drums in the hollow undercuts.

We covered a quarter mile of one bank and crossed over to return upstream along the other bank. Crossing required that we find shallow water at the tail of a pool, which meant we had to convince around seventy or eighty head of buffalo to leave the cool waters. When we moved toward them, it was our good fortune that the old bull who stood watch walked away, followed by the herd. As we crossed our boots sank into the muddy river bottom churned up by the bison.

We headed back upstream. A delicious stretch of deadfalls looked very inviting. Had there been bass in Slough Creek I would have wagered that the biggest ones lurked there. Before I had a chance to observe this, Melinda said, "If I were a big trout I would hang out right there."

"You mean here?" I said as I splatted down my fly (a Dave's Hopper). I intended for Melinda to take a shot. Wouldn't you know it? The hopper landed and a huge cutthroat rose from beneath the log. I knew, Melinda knew, and the trout knew that there would be no point in putting any more flies on that calm water. Of course I missed the fish. Melinda said it was no big thing, but I never forgot it.

FALL RIVER TROUT

———◆———

If you drift down a mile of the Fall River you will pass 3,500 trout. You may not catch 3,500 fish. You may not catch any. Just like everywhere else, you have to know what you're doing. You have to learn special techniques, the cycles of insect life, the rhythm of the seasons, days, wind, and weather. Get to know the river, though, and you should take your share of trout.

The setting is a wide valley in southern California guarded by a ring of mountains, most of them volcanic. Mt. Lassen is on one side and Mt. Shasta, more distant, rises on the other. Even in summer their peaks are topped with snow. Closer in, Soldier Mountain watches over the river. The valley, flat as a table, sits on a bed of lava. Alluvial soil covers the lava. Marsh grass and tule reeds provide most of the vegetation, with an occasional tree to break up the vista. The wildlife includes ducks and geese, coots, herons, eagles, ospreys, muskrats, and deer.

The river starts as snow on the mountaintops, melting and seeping down through the limestone and lava, collecting underground, flowing toward the valley floor through a series of natural tunnels and tubes in the volcanic rock. At places these tubes ascend to the surface, bubbling up as springs. The Fall River is born of 1,000 such springs. It is slow-moving, nutrient-rich, and full of life.

There is a providential impurity in the water that prevents the stocking of foreign strains of rainbow trout. The local rainbows, though, are highly resistant to many diseases. For this reason the trout from the nearby McCloud River were the broodstock for the transplanting of rainbows to the East by Robert Barnwell Roosevelt in the 1870s. Brown trout, too, have found their way into the system, but they comprise barely five percent of the population. When you catch a Fall River rainbow, you know that he comes from untold generations of native fish.

The Achumawi Indians lived here first. They hunted deer with bow and arrow. They caught ducks in nooses strung over the river and trout in their fish traps. Life was bountiful for the Achumawi until the arrival of the white settlers. Then the trouble started, as recounted in the old county histories that tell of a "massacrec" here, an ambush there, of burnings, beatings, rapes, and looting, of young children who went berry picking and never returned. Inevitably, the government sent in the cavalry, with the result that the settlers kept the lion's share and the Indians were given their allotments, which they hold to this day.

Having fought so long and hard, having lived in the shadow of death and danger for so many years, the landowners felt very strongly about the sacred rights of private property. Their barbed-wire fences extended across the river. If you wanted to fish the Fall, you had to know somebody.

Or you needed a pair of wire cutters. In 1969 a certain Judge Barr, from Eureka, slipped his boat into the river and proceeded to cut every piece of wire he found, thereby attracting the attention of shotgun-toting locals. But the judge's logic was compelling. Insofar as navigable waterways could not

be legally obstructed, and insofar as Judge Barr's boat was proof of the navigability of the Fall, the barriers came down.

Once word got out and the crowds showed up, that could have been the end of the great fishing on the Fall. But California Trout (CalTrout), an excellent organization, led the fight to preserve this fishery, in part by pressuring the state to lower the limit to two fish per day. And it promoted a Wild Trout Program that forsakes stocking and calls for stream management on a natural-reproduction basis.

I first fished the Fall with Mike Michalak. This was in the early years of his now-famous outfitting company, The Fly Shop in Redding, California. On that maiden voyage we arrived right after a spinner fall. There is nothing more subtle nor delicate than the sip of a trout feeding on spinners. It is almost not there, more implied than actual. The water barely shivers, but there is something in our hunter-gatherer genome that can take the measure of such ephemera. The river was full of big trout and all of them were feeding. However, catching such fish—amidst a carpet of floating food in clear calm water—is one of fly-fishing's most captivating, often frustrating, challenges.

In such conditions, if you tried the traditional upstream cast, one of two things would ensue. The impact of your line on the calm water would scare a number of trout, if not the whole school. Even a cast as light as a sigh would still have put leader over the trout before it saw the fly. Again a sure trout scatterer.

Mike introduced me to the inelegantly named dump cast, which works as follows. Preparatory to your first cast, you strip out 40 or 50 feet of line,

after which you lay down a short cast, about 20 feet. Don't worry that your fly is still 30 feet from your fish; all you're doing here is placing the fly precisely in the feeding lane. Next lift your rod tip to straighten out the line and leader. This will ensure that the fly is the first piece of tackle to pass into the trout's window of vision.

Now, for the finesse part. The trick is to keep the fly unaffected by anything but the current while maintaining contact with the fly. This requires that you pay line out through the tip top in a motion similar to the way basketball players used to shoot the underhanded foul shot. Although under normal circumstances you like a little slack in the line to compensate for micro-currents, the take of a trout is so subtle on the Fall that you need to come tight, immediately yet gently.

I practiced until I got the hang of it and set my fly down in the middle of a large group of spinners. Mike advised that this was exactly wrong.

"Think about it," he said, "If there are 100 flies going by together and yours is among them, those aren't very good betting odds, especially when yours is the only phony in the pack. What you want to do is false cast until there's some space between groups of flies. Hit that spot and start dumping line. If you're in his feeding lane, he'll take."

I did as I was told. Somehow I didn't connect. It takes some practice to pick your fly out of the surface glare. When you do, it's incredibly exciting because you know just where the fish is so that you get those long moments of expectation as the fly passes over the mark. It's somewhat like bird hunting when you know a grouse is going to flush and that you're going to have to react. If you can't see what's happening, however, you're out of luck. You will strike, as I did, when there's no fish, and you will fail to strike when a fish takes. You just have to stay with it until you get it.

Then the wind started to blow. It comes up strong at some point every day during summer, and there's nothing you can do but find yourself a lee or wrap it up until afternoon. We chose the latter course.

Back at Lava Creek Lodge, the barometer told a tale of woe. We mixed up some hot cocoa, poured in a couple of fingers of amaretto, and topped it with whipped cream. We sat in a row at the bar, hands on chin, elbows on the counter. Soldier Mountain was wreathed, funereally, in rain, fog, mist, wind, and more rain. We stared at the fire, convincing ourselves that it beat working—but every so often one of us got unconvinced. We took turns pacing, tapping the barometer, staring outside.

The plan was to wait it out and hope things cleared off for sunset. Part-time guide Dennis Swope had promised to take me out to fish the Hex hatch—Hex, as in *Hexagenia limbata*, an enormous drake (just like in the Adirondacks) whose emergence catches the attention of big trout and causes them to feed recklessly.

Swope is a man who has his fishing priorities in order. Before he moved to the Fall, he worked for the Safeway Supermarket chain in San Francisco. However, once he discovered the Fall and its sister rivers, Hat Creek and the McCloud, he found himself spending twelve hours each weekend driving from home to fishing and back, at which point he reached a life decision as he took a job as the nighttime stock manager at a Safeway near the Fall—working all night so he could fish during the day.

We needed a little cooperation from the elements. They obliged with a rainbow arching across the sky, rising from the lower river. We took it for divine intervention and headed to the river, arriving in time to watch the clouds and rain roll back in. I can't tell you how many times in my life a hatch of drakes has shown every sign of coming off, and then the wind came up or it turned cold or fog rolled in or the trout hadn't read the script and didn't know that such times signal the greatest feeding frenzy of the year. I can tell you that having driven the aggregate of a few thousand miles in pursuit of Hexes and Green Drakes, I have never really hit it. The Fall River that night was par for the course. No sooner had we arrived than the black storm clouds did too and the few Hexes on the water closed up shop.

But the Fall also has a saving grace. When the scuds overwhelm the food source on a grass bed they will blow off it en masse and float downstream to more plentiful pastures. So as we desultorily tossed nymphs in the hopes of catching fish, the scuds set themselves adrift and the water turned frothy with feeding trout.

Dennis and I tied on Zug Bugs and fished them down and across, the old-fashioned way. I took a three-pounder, which was the biggest trout of my life to that point. Understandably, I never held it against the Fall that she had saved her Hexes for another trip.

SILVER CREEK

I remember my first look at Silver Creek. It was forty miles, about an hour's drive from the green highlands of Sun Valley. To get there you must run the gauntlet of speed traps in Hailey, Bellevue, and Gannett, snaking your way through a range of brown hills—an unforgiving moonscape relieved only by thickets of sage. Closer to the creek, tumbleweed gives way to fields of ripe barley. In season the bottomland is covered with swaths of flowers that were surely were named by poets—panic grass, hound's-tongue, death camas, and pearly everlasting. And then, the marvelous spring creek itself, running its course through the verdant valley looking, not surprisingly, like a long ribbon of silver.

Just below, you will see Sullivan's Slough—its shallow flat water calm and apparently undisturbed by fish, until you realize that the large dark shapes on the bottom are not rocks, but rather what the locals call "slobs"—huge representatives of the pure strain of McCloud River rainbows, introduced at the turn of the century. They replaced the native cutthroats that could not abide the change in habitat brought about by the settlers whose plows chewed up the low ground and whose cattle trampled down the riverbanks.

Then, just downstream of the slough, there is a mile-long meander that cuts through the land of the Nature Conservancy, a preservation organization that has sought to create a forever-wild haven on the upper reaches of the creek. The conservancy water ends at a medium-sized impoundment that receives a lot of fishing pressure, but which still holds many good trout. There's a dam at the end of the pond, marking the beginning of the Purdy Ranch. The stretch of water that follows is, to my mind, the best place to fill up on the Silver Creek experience. Bobbing along in a float tube, you enter the stream just below the conservancy. Once in the water, you don't get out for the six or seven hours that it takes to traverse the Purdy Ranch. The creek itself is considered a navigable waterway, so it is open to the public. The banks, however, are private and posted.

If you hit the Purdy stretch right, you will cast to rising fish all day. I hit it on such a day. There were five of us: Clay Carter, Andy Kent, and Ron Fudge made up the Sun Valley contingent, three dyed-in-the-wool fisherman who will probably miss their own funerals if there is a hatch on; and myself and Tony Atwill, a *Sports Afield* contributing editor and my frequent fishing companion in years past.

Tony and I arrived at the access early and chatted with the other fishermen. There was talk of streams all over the West. A Florida couple had just helicoptered in from Jackson Hole, where the water was high and the hatches late. They planned to fish Silver Creek in the morning, after which they were going to West Yellowstone for the afternoon. In this fashion they were going to fish their way to Alaska by fall.

In contrast to the well-equipped Floridians, two fellows in a beat-up Dodge rolled in from Henry's Fork, having driven half the night. They sported two-day stubbles and looked as if they were not above eating beans from a can. They filled us in on conditions at the Railroad Ranch. And so on. Each morning you can count on getting a nationwide fishing report if you hang out long enough by the Nature Conservancy pond. You stand there on the

bridge, sip coffee, and ease into the day.

We finally got geared up and moving by 9:30 A.M., an ungainly armada of four anglers in float tubes and one (Atwill) in an inflatable boat. We eased across the pond and portaged the dam, re-entering the creek at the beginning of the Purdy Ranch. The Trico spinners were just hitting the water, dense clouds of tiny black mayflies. The fish rose in groups of nine or ten, sipping and swirling.

At such times, the fish are so insistent in their feeding that there is no putting them down. Even the careless caster is forgiven by the trout of Silver Creek. If the fish sees line, he won't take on that cast; however, he'll take on the next if it's properly presented.

As we entered the water, I could see downstream for one hundred yards. Thirty or forty fish were breaking the surface with regularity. I tied on a #22 spinner imitation with a black body, long tails, and white wings. We spread out, each of us casting to groups of nine or ten risers. Clay hooked one and let go an ear-cracking whoop. Andy stalked a beautiful trout and took it on the twentieth cast. Then Ron had one on, then Clay again, then Tony, then me. On and on for three hours.

The Trico spinner fall ended and *Callibaetis* began to hatch. They covered my hat, my arms, my glasses. The trout never missed a beat. They kept on feeding. We fished. We chatted. We floated. We traded techniques. We swapped flies. We sweated in the sun.

Then there were more spinners, gold and purple PMDs. Floating, bobbing, and casting as the gentle current pulled us along, we were like weightless astronauts. Time passed as seamlessly as I can ever recall; a peaceful dream punctuated by the lunge of a hooked trout, the whir of the reel, the click, click of the drag.

We stopped for a bite and took turns casting to a large bank feeder. As, one after the other, we failed to interest the big old trout, we kidded each other, like guys at a country fair taking turns trying to ring the bell with a sledgehammer. Along the bank, an old man let fly beautiful casts, the whole width of the stream. Each time he hooked a fish, his golden retriever jumped and barked. By the time the PMDs quit, the thermometer had passed ninety and I was drenched in sweat, the kind of sweat that wants a cold beer.

We climbed out of the stream and went to a welcoming bar—dark and cool inside, with bracing air conditioning and the perfume of ice-cold beer. I bought a draft from Mickey—no last name, just Mickey. She turned out prodigious cheeseburgers and knew everything that has happened on Silver Creek for the past half century: how Averill Harriman, chairman of the Union Pacific Railroad, built the glittering Sun Valley resort. How Gary Cooper and Clark Gable, Jane Russell, John Wayne, and, most of all, Ernest Hemingway made it a fashionable destination for the Smart Set.

One evening during my stay in Idaho, I went to the stream to meet up with Harry Wilson, the entrepreneur who founded the Scott rod company. Scotts were the first of the precision-made, high-performance graphite rods. Their castability was, to be sure, a function of design, but no less a product of Harry's exigent nature: "I reject nine out of ten blanks," he told me with pride.

Ever since I discovered his rods, we had developed a phone friendship, and when I told him that I was going to Silver Creek, he revealed his plan to be there at the same time.

He was a portly man, probably in his early seventies at the time. When we rendezvoused I had brought along an extra float tube so that Harry could join me for the evening rise on the conservancy water.

"Don't know if I want to try that," Harry said. "I've never done it before and I don't like the looks of it."

When I told him that there was no other way to reach the line of rising fish up against the tule reeds, he said, "What the hell?" at which point I received a lesson about fly fishing that I find ever more comforting with the passing years. You see, Harry looked hopeless as he tried to step into the tube and even worse as he held it up around his waist and hobbled down to the stream, like a tipsy ballerina holding up a wet tutu.

Harry was not that spry to begin with and in the new gear he was positively ungainly. But then, when he was afloat in the water, the years melted away. Unsteadiness on land is not a problem when you are floating in calm water. Harry clearly enjoyed the experience and, better yet, his old man's doddering was transformed into the elegant motions of a crisp and powerful caster. One after another, his casts shot out, sixty feet each time. In ten minutes Harry hooked four great fish. My goal in life, ever since that night, is to be able to cast like Harry when I am seventy, and my second goal is to remember, as Harry showed me, that you're never too old to try something new if it means good fishing.

BUMBY ON THE LITTLE WOOD

———◆———

If you would like to keep a fishing spot to yourself, one of the best ways I know is to drop a poisonous snake reference into your conversation. Though I have had four confirmed viper sightings in my whole life (and two of them were in Africa), I have certainly imagined them to be in hundreds of places.

People will pretend that they are blasé about it, but they're not. Take a northerner down south, and he will ask, in the most offhanded (but visibly terrified way), "Uh . . . like I don't really care a lot . . . uh, just curious . . . uh, are there any poisonous snakes you have to look out for? . . . just in case . . . not that I'm worried at all." They're not fooling anybody—they are as sure that Alabama is teeming with copperheads and moccasins as Alabamans are that every street corner in New York harbors a mugger.

Jack Hemingway, Papa Hemingway's eldest son, was well aware of this phenomenon and used it to safeguard a favorite spot on the Little Wood River.

"Not too many people come here," he said. "It has a reputation for rattlesnakes, and I have done nothing to counter such talk."

"And?" I said.

"And what?"

"And, are there rattlesnakes?"

"Well . . . yeah . . . you see their skins on the ground after they shed, but I never saw an actual snake."

We had driven to the Valley of the Little Wood in Jack's big, beautiful van. We had become

friends while working on a film about Papa in Cuba. The idea was that we would hang out with Papa's old buddies, have a cocktail or two in his old haunts, and fish with his number-one fishing partner, Gregorio Fuentes (who just recently died at the age of 106 after successfully defying and outliving the doctors who told him to give up cigars and rum). During that trip Jack confessed that he didn't care much for marlin fishing, which involved a lot of trolling. I concurred and the two of us forged a fly-rodding bond as we trolled flies in hopes of pounding up a mahi or two. We enjoyed ourselves in Cuba, in part I suspect because the survivors of the old days took Bumby's visit (everybody in Havana called Jack by this childhood nickname) as a pretext to party as heartily as Fidel would allow.

Jack had not been back to Cuba since before the Bay of Pigs. Returning brought out stories buried by a half century of history. Like, for instance, how in all the years that his father had gone out marlin hunting with Jack, he only let his son take the rod once. Or how they used to put a dead chicken on the roof of their home, Finca la Vigía, and then, when the buzzards came in for a bite, Jack and Papa would practice their wing shooting on the vultures. Or how, whenever Papa came back from being lionized by the literary world, he would get in shape for big-game fishing by sitting in a chair next to the swimming pool and using a broomstick to raise and lower a five-gallon bucket of water into and out of the pool. He would spend two weeks at this, an hour a day.

We had to leave Cuba in a rush. It was the day that America invaded Grenada. Things were pretty weird in Havana, so we got out of town. Jack and I stayed in touch, made a few fishing plans that fell through, and, with one thing and another, here we were on our way to the Little Wood.

Before they donated the property to the state, the Hemingway family had owned the five-acre stretch that we were going to fish. Compared to the verdant valley of Silver Creek, the Little Wood was a desert with a slice of water running through it. Pretty water, though. Jack led me to a favorite stretch. Nonchalantly, I checked out the ground as we walked (looking for rattlesnake signs). I waded into the river and Jack walked upstream to fish. As I try to recapture the image of that afternoon, everything is suffused with gold. The yellow-brown rocks, the yellowing summer shrubs, the water shooting off reflections of the brilliant sunlight. Combine glinting yellowness with the *shh . . . shh . . .* of rushing

water and my keen concentration on the white tuft of my Parachute Adams, it was all quite hypnotic. Hooking and landing three of the four fat fifteen-inch brown trout that rose to my fly stirred me briefly from my reverie.

"Good going," Jack said, as I released my last fish of the day.

On the way home we pulled over at the vista offered by a mountain pass. Such sights often bring out the philosophical side of people, and Jack held forth on catch-and-release angling, a practice that we both championed, but which neither of us accorded the status of religious doctrine in which many anglers hold it. He had thought a lot about the issue.

"I release my trout, but I have nothing against killing trout," he said. "I have killed my share. The thing is, because they are predators high up in the food chain, their numbers are small when compared to their prey. Even a little bit of pressure can turn a great fishery into nothing special. If you like to catch trout, it makes great practical sense to release your fish, but you lose me when you start to bring morality into the picture. Release your fish, and leave it at that."

There was not much that I could add beyond, "I agree."

"My dad and I used to come up here with our shotguns and shoot pigeons as they came through the pass, back when there was an open season," Jack recalled. "And I remember one night sitting here with Papa, watching a mountain lion down in the valley. I am certain my dad would have shot it if he could, even though it would have been against the law. Papa made up his own rules."

THE GOLDEN RULE

———◆———

*G*olden Trout Creek is in the highest Sierras, where green meadows warm to the sun and where Mt. Whitney stands watch—shaggy, jaggy, and rimmed with never-melting snow. The scenery alone would warrant a visit, but for anglers it is even more special because that most beautiful trout, *Oncorhyncus mykiss aquabonita* or golden trout, is native only to this one drainage. A relative of the rainbow and the cutthroat, its forebears no doubt found refuge there in the last Ice Age. The same story could once have been told of other unique trout in the flowages of the West Coast, but man or nature has excused almost all of them from the scene.

The golden trout, though, remains, which is why I took a twin-engine Cessna from Inyokern, at the edge of the desert, up to the meadows where Golden Trout Creek rises. In summer the days are hot, and the sun unrelenting, but the nights at 10,300 feet can be brisk and the creeks often freeze over in the morning even in summer. In the early misty hours, the smell of pine balsam fills the air, unconfused by any other scent. On such mornings, you might hear the hoofbeats of horses running toward the corral and see the sun behind them lighting up their manes like clouds.

On my first morning, the sunbeams licked the frost from the sage as I dipped my water jug in the creek and drank my fill. "Cares and woes be damned," I thought. "This is going to be a hell of a day."

After two mugs of coffee, I tucked some cheese and bread in my sack and headed down a dusty path, over a hill, and into the valley of Golden Trout Creek. Trout rose all around: at the tail and lip of every pool, tight to the bank, and out in midstream. I took this as my cue to fish.

One after another, the trout came to my fly, no matter which fly I tried. The trout were disposed to hit anything that looked like food. I cast forehand, underhand, and backhand. I tied on the longest, lightest leader I could handle and snapped off some crisp roll casts. I cast to many risers and I cast to fish whose presence I only sensed. When they didn't take, I knew I had done something wrong. A perfect cast brought a strike every time. Sloppiness brought refusal.

Working my way upstream, I came upon a series of waterfalls. Each pool held trout and I fished them all, dapping as best I could. Suddenly I drew up short, frozen to the spot like a dog on point. Unmindful of my presence, a positively gorgeous ten-inch golden finned in the upwelling froth of the cascade, darting here and there to intercept some tumbling food. Hemmed in by the boulders, shaded by overhanging boughs, she was uncatchable. She had color to spare. Blues deep as seawater and paler than steam. Dots—or were they reflections?—of forest green ran from gill to tail. A gash of burning red down her flanks. The brilliant markings from which her species draws its name were as big and as shiny as doubloons: honest-to-god, take-it-to-the-bank gold.

I took four fish and put them on a stringer tied to my belt so the trout trailed in the water, alive. I found a quiet pool, deep and sunlit, took my clothes off, and jumped in. On the shore, a ring of volcanic rocks, with ashes in the center, told of other pilgrims to this same sunny spot.

Gathering some wood took no time at all. The fire caught with equal speed. I gutted the fish, skewered them on a branch, and grilled them. In the space of two minutes they crossed from life to death, from gold to fire-black. When I had eaten, I tossed the skeletons into the fire.

The next day I met Bob, the cowboy. He was camped with his wife, their teenage daughter, and the daughter's love-struck suitor. No doubt they had seen my buddy, Frank McKevitt, and I approaching on horseback. Our camp lay nine miles upstream at Tunnel Meadows, nine butt-chafing miles for those of us who don't ride horses too often.

Bob's camp on Whitney Meadow looked pretty as a painting, the kind you don't buy because no one will believe it, it's so perfect. We tethered our horses in the shade and set about fishing, mindlessly chugging along, content as two fat bees in a bouquet of roses. Cowboy Bob appeared out of nowhere, with the daughter's boyfriend in tow. They were resting on the opposite bank. I nodded and continued to fish, trying to look casual. I just couldn't resist putting on a little casting exhibition, and I actually looked pretty good until I started playing with more line than I could handle. Ah, vanity!

"I see you like to fly-fish," Bob said. Given the situation, it was hard to back off from that kind of conversation opener. So we talked. I showed him how to use my fly rod and he wasn't too bad with it.

We strolled up to his camp. While sipping some coffee, I learned that Bob was in the horse business. As we moved on to pan biscuits and eggs, I learned that the horse business isn't any more paved with gold than any other business and that even cowboys have to get away from it all sometimes. Bob's daughter suggested that I might care for some trout. Eager to please, the boyfriend took his cue, bounded down to the stream, and lifted a stringer that must have held twenty trout.

At that particular moment—having grilled up my catch the day before—I didn't feel in command of the moral artillery to lecture Bob on catch-and-release. Four trout, twenty trout, what's the difference? I don't think Bob or any of his party would have put much stock in the argument that my meal was a "ritual," a "communion," a "rite of passage." It may have been all of that, but it was also lunch, and I'm sure Bob would have called it that.

"Bob," I said, "how come you don't fish farther on downstream where the trout are really big?" Between the lines I was implying that they were more suitable for eating.

He waved his hand in disgust: "Too many German browns."

That was a new one on me. Once, in the writings of Ray Bergman, I had read of some salty New Hampshire old-timer who had expressed a preference for smallmouth over "trashy German browns." But in this day and age, we all know that the brown trout is highly regarded, even preferred. He is crafty. He grows to great size. He rises well to the fly. In his fishlike way, he plays the game properly. But he is not a native American.

In the natural scheme of things the rainbow trout rules the West. The brookie holds sway in the East. The brown trout was put in our waters by man, a fact that had not escaped my cowpoke friend. Like me, he had been drawn to this meadow by the desire to find something original, ancient, and wild. And though I was one kind of fisherman and he another, we weren't opposites. He knew and I knew that we would never catch a big fish in those waters. Big was for other waters. The golden trout is a jewel, and jewels are never big; they are beautiful. I just wished he wouldn't take so many.

"Bob, why do you suppose those trout have so much gold in them?" I asked.

"Because," he said, "they live nearest to the sun."

IN PRAISE OF UNFAMOUS RIVERS

———◆———

*I*n *southern Wyoming, the high plains outside Laramie climb past the tree line to the cold peaks of the* Medicine Bow Wilderness. Halfway down the road to the old mining town of Centennial you can pull off the highway and see the ancient ruts of the Overland Trail, where the Conestoga wagons of the early settlers left their mark. This is cattle country with far-flung homesteads and snaking lines of willows and cottonwoods marking the meandering courses of the no-name streams that feed into the Laramie River. In our era of famous rivers and famous anglers, anonymity is a great attraction. And so it was with great anticipation that I accepted the invitation of Gary Edwards and his wife, Robin, to explore the little known but highly praised waters around Laramie.

Our first stop was an old ranch outside Centennial where four generations of the same family occupied a compound fanning out from a sturdy prairie farmhouse built by their Swedish ancestor in 1914. It was still inhabited by his bright-eyed ninety-six-year-old widow, who had survived thirty-nine years of teaching fourth-graders and who napped every afternoon so that she could watch *David Letterman* each night. It was hay-making time. Her son, Perry, and his son, Jimmy, were along with their wives, bringing in winter food for their cattle. The herd was in summer pasture up in the Medicine Bow Wilderness.

After a cholesterol-rich breakfast Gary and I took the ranch's old pickup truck (230,000 miles and still counting) and drove across ten miles of back roads to a neighboring ranch and a little meadow stream. The strong wet smell of fresh mint rose from the stream

bank. A cloud covered the sun. The shade felt good. The stream was full of waving watercress that set up a web of drag-inducing currents.

Three trout rose in the channel. Steady sipping rises. I cast a Griffith's Gnat. On the second cast a trout took. I pulled back as hard as I could, and my 6X tippet held. The trout bore for cover. I held his head up, maneuvered him around the weeds, and unhooked him: sixteen inches, fat from freshwater shrimp, and nicely spotted. The monkey was now off my back. I'd gotten a trout right off the bat, the best way to start a fishing day.

As we walked, we flushed an army of hoppers, so I switched to a hopper imitation on slightly stronger tippet. We crossed the stream. I saw a rise and cast. Just then, I heard a fierce whinnying sound, as a horse who had been grazing behind me took off with a start. I could see the wakes of terrified trout as the horse's clattering hooves pounded out a tom-tom beat along the deeply undercut bank.

"Cast into the channel by the weed line. There has to be a brown trout there where the currents come together," Gary said.

I cast. Pow! I had one on. He made for cover. I reared back. He broke off.

We continued upstream. We saw many fish. They would rise on the first cast or they wouldn't rise at all. A flock of pelicans flew overhead. Pelicans? It turns out these birds do indeed inhabit the high plains. Just then I heard a sound like snare drums, thousands of them getting louder and louder. I looked up. Rainclouds. The sound was that of rain-drops hitting the metal roofs of the ranch's out-buildings. We raced back to the car just ahead of the cloudburst. The morning's fishing was done.

We passed the house of Harry Bath, who was, I learned, one of the four Bath brothers. They regularly placed first, second, third, and fourth in the annual chuck-wagon race, which is the grand finale of the rodeo, known as Cheyenne's Frontier Days. Getting a chuck wagon to do a wheelie is an art most like that of Roman chariot driving. And since there aren't many Roman chariot drivers around any more these days, when it came time to make the movie *Ben Hur*, the film's producers offered the Baths a good paycheck to drive the chariots in the demolition derby that was the famous action sequence in the film. "We shaved the axles so when you make contact you'll crash and lose your wheels. Don't worry, it's safe," the producers said. Three weeks later, when the Baths were released from the hospital, they came home to Centennial.

We returned to the ranch, drank from the bott-omless pot of coffee in the kitchen, and took a short snooze before heading out for the evening's fishing. As we climbed into the truck, Gary lay a pistol and holster on the seat next to him.

"Mountain lions," he explained.

We drove through freshly mown fields and around thickets of willow until we reached the stream. We crossed it on foot and climbed a hill on the far bank. From the summit we could see clear across the green plain. There was hay everywhere, piled in bales, wound into huge rolls, dumped loose into large bins. Had the rain that now bore down on us arrived two weeks earlier, it would have been welcomed as a blessing. Now all it could do was make the hay harder to handle and prone to rot.

We continued along the high tableland. After a mile or two of fence hopping we descended again to the stream, keeping a weather eye out for the thunderstorm. We crossed one meander, then another, detouring around a series of beaver dams.

The stream was thirty feet across at its widest, bordered by willows, and wherever there was enough timber, impounded by beavers. It looped in wide lazy arcs. We approached a deep, flat pool behind an old beaver dam and looked for risers. Gary picked his way atop the remains of the dam. Just then I saw a rise where the current drove into the bank.

"Stop," I commanded and Gary stopped, balancing precariously.

"Upstream, thirty feet, right in the bubble line against the near bank."

In the angled light of late afternoon Gary couldn't see a thing. He would have to fly by my radar. He stripped out what he judged to be thirty feet of line and laid it into the current below the busted dam. He steadied himself as best he could and sent his Elk Hair Caddis sailing.

"Short, Gary. Five feet more and a little closer to the bank."

It took two more casts before his fly settled in the sweet spot of the foam line. The trout took. Gary raised his rod and fought the fish while working equally hard to keep from falling off the dam. He brought to mind a frantic orchestra conductor. He released the fish, a plump brown. "Sometimes trout fishing is a two-man job," he said.

I walked upstream, standing in mid-current. I took two nice fish on a Dave's Hopper. The thunderstorm rumbled in the distance and, between us and it, a rainbow soared across the plains, glowing against the dark clouds. The stream, still in sunlight, took a sharp turn left, and I heard, but could not see, a trout feeding just around the corner. I whipped a cast upstream of where I judged the sound to be and he took violently and with much commotion. I came tight to him and felt the head shakes of a really good fish. He made for the undercut on the far bank.

"Rod in the water," Gary counseled. I pointed my rod tip down and finally pulled the trout out from his refuge. We measured him against my rod, nineteen inches and broad shouldered. He was a uniquely satisfying trout. I unhooked him and watched him finning in the current until he melted back into grassy bottom.

We dined in Centennial that night at the Old Corral steakhouse, where they serve a fifty-four-ounce steak. A husband-and-wife musician team, "Jeannie and Will," accompanied by a vigorous drum machine, led a crowd-pleasing sing-along of "Beer Barrel Polka." A banner across the stage proclaimed that Jeannie and Will had appeared at the Old Corral for "twenty-five straight years."

"I'm Royce, I'll be your waiter tonight," a young man said, more New Age than Old West. I ordered a shell steak and a martini.

The next morning, Gary, Robin, and I drove into the Medicine Bow Wilderness, passing through ten thousand feet along a cliff-hugging, switchback road. We parked and walked a half mile to a cabin that Perry kept up there for those days when he went to check on his cattle in their summer pasture.

I approached a beaver pond, maybe a hundred feet across. I stood below the dam and looked, voyeuristically, into the pond. I cast to an inviting rise. A pretty brookie struck with brio. I brought him in quickly and put him in my creel. I took two more from that pond and then moved on. I began to try casting into narrow channels, overhung with grass and branches, very challenging. There were brook trout everywhere you might expect to find one. A cool breeze brought the bracing scent of sage. Black clouds boiled over the mountains. Thunder boomed in the distance. We began to fish our way back. Lightning cleaved the sky on our side of the nearest peak. We made a beeline for the cabin.

While I made a fire, Robin chopped the potatoes and onions and Gary cleaned the fish in the cold spring near the cabin. Robin melted bacon fat in the pan, browned the onions, and threw in the potatoes with plenty of salt and pepper. She didn't turn them until they were well crisped on the bottom. Next, she placed some halved tomatoes into the skillet and grilled them until they were hot and soft. Finally she floured the trout and fried them in the bacon grease. The small trout curled right away. The rain began to fall, just a few drops at first. When the trout were done, we retreated into the cabin. The lighting came closer and closer. I never heard louder thunder. When the rain finally busted loose, it filled the cabin with rat-a-tat of fat raindrops on the old wooden shingles. The air was cold. The food was hot, and we were quite happy to eat and watch the summer storm work its way across the valley.

The little shack was tucked into a pine grove at the head of a valley full of beaver ponds stretching as far as the horizon. We walked through the woods for about a mile and then cut through a warren of berry bushes and not-always-visible beaver channels that made for unsure footing and slow going.

"8X and little flies," Gary observed. "Start casting near the dams and then work your way up."

Brook Trout with Rosti Potatoes

Francis Mallmann is Argentina's most famous, and in my books, coolest chef. The guy drips style. My family and I spent Easter week with him in his cabin in the absolute remotest part of Patagonia. It was a ten-hour drive and a one-hour boat ride to the prettiest place on earth (at least I have never seen anything to surpass it): a gin-clear lake surrounded by a lush mountain forest towered over by the snow-peaked Andes. Francis cooked all of our meals on a big cast-iron grill under which he placed the glowing embers from a roaring campfire. At the time he made this dish, I hadn't killed a trout for twenty years. But Francis's lake, which is hardly ever fished, is loaded with trout dying of old age. For my younger daughter, Lily, it was the first time that she had donned her waders and actually tied into some real trout. Lucky kid, I thought, to have played her first "big league" game in such a beautiful ballpark.

Serves 4

Brook Trout

4 large Idaho potatoes, scrubbed
2 brook trout (2 pounds each or 4
1-pound trout) filleted, skin on
Salt
Freshly ground black pepper
¼ cup unsalted butter

Heat a large cast-iron pan, griddle, or Teflon frying pan over medium heat. Melt half the butter in the pan. Coarsely grate 2 of the potatoes. Place the grated potatoes in the pan in a 1-inch-thick layer. Season the fillets with salt and pepper and place on top of the potatoes. Grate the remaining 2 potatoes and place them on top of the fillets. Continue cooking the potatoes for a total of 15 minutes, or until golden brown on the bottom. With the help of plate turn over the potatoes as you would an upside-down cake. Add the remaining butter to the pan, and when melted slide the potatoes and trout carefully into the pan, uncooked side down. Cook the second side for 10 to 12 minutes, until golden brown. Cut as you would a pie and serve with a green salad.

Note: When you grate the potatoes, don't touch or move them too much,
and place them carefully in the pan. This will give them a nicer texture and look when they are done.
It's important to cook this dish over medium heat; if the heat is too high,
the outside will crisp up too soon and the inside will remain raw.

THE MIGHTY MO

Although I am often asked the question, it is hard to pick the Best Trout Stream. Best for what? Dry fly?
Biggest fish? Prettiest? Easiest? The master of ceremonies at the Miss America pageant used
to dodge such questions with something like "Gee, all the contestants are so pretty, it's going
to be really hard to pick a winner."

The plain facts of the matter are that on any given day a great stream can be a bust and,
by the same token, a so-so stream might produce the fishing of a lifetime. Still, if pressed, I
would not hem and haw for very long before admitting a partiality to the Missouri, specifically
the stretch below Three Rivers, Montana. Issuing from Holter Dam and carrying with it the
waters of the Madison, Jefferson, and Gallatin Rivers, this tailwater fishery is rich in nutri-
ents and remains trout-pleasingly cool even in the blazing summer sun. For me, prolific
hatches, trout rising rhythmically to emergers, duns, and spinners, and seductively slurpy
rise forms induce a trancelike epiphany. The living haze of clouds of flies blowing off the
water; the sweet, almost soundless gulp of feeding trout, their shadowy forms undulating in
the current; the waving beds of green river grass; and of course the clear, clear water—so
clear that everything happens in plain sight. All of this I find impossibly seductive.

So I go with the Missouri, although some by-the-book traditionalists prefer the free-
flowing Yellowstone or upper Madison, dismissing tailwaters as trout fishing's version of a
silicone implant. In the recesses of my angling soul, I even concede that they might have a
point. But if casting to rising wild fish in calm water haunts your dreams—as it does mine—

there is nothing I know of that surpasses this giant spring creek.

I may love the Missouri, but she does not always love me. In fact the first time I fished her, I received the comeuppance that seems to follow whenever a good fishing session gets you to thinking that you have become a tip-top angler. I had been fishing on—let's call it Kitty Creek (because that is not its name). It is a smallish river that receives very little pressure, so my casts frequently summoned a fierce strike from a fat, healthy, stream-borne brown.

I was so successful (as were my fishing partners, Larry Aiuppy and Doug McClelland) that I began to think that I had broken through to a new level of angling prowess.

Flushed with success, we drove back along the valley of the Missouri: a curvy band of green and gold. We were not in a rush. The afternoon was hot. The sun glinted off the stream in that high-summer way that I have come to realize means there is no point in fishing until the shadows lengthen. When they did, the flies appeared on cue. First came legions of frantic caddis, anarchically break-dancing all over the surface. Lots of activity, but the flies stayed about three inches above the water, and all the trout could do was look up greedily like a kid with two cents in his pocket contemplating cookies in a bakery window.

Then . . . a rise. And another. Then two more. No question about it, we were moving into a hatch. Doug, Larry, and I wadered up and made our way into the stream. We each staked out a micro current.

The trout were eager, but not reckless. I tied on size 22 this and 24 that. I went to my go-to fly for small hatches (a size 20 Griffith's Gnat). Although I considered an upstream cast to be out of the question, just above me a very fat rainbow trout pushed about three inches of snout out of the water as it inhaled a mouthful of little white flies. I aimed a slack cast slightly to the right of the fish. I figured I had a fifty percent chance of the leader curling to the left, and happily it did so. The trout rose, its take as gentle as the fall of a leaf on the water. I struck, feeling the

weight of a strong fish. I put some bend in the rod to keep the trout out of the grass bed to its left and, in consequence, ten seconds after I hooked him, he had broken me off. Doug and Larry had similar luck—or lack of it. We fished for three hours, until we could no longer see the rises (long before that our little flies had become invisible). I did the math. Collectively we had about eighty years of trout-fishing experience, yet in those three hours we had each succeeded in hooking and quickly losing one fish apiece.

So much for my notion that I had moved up into the ranks of gifted anglers. But getting shut out on the Missouri when you are casting to tauntingly rising fish is exciting, even exhilarating. I had to make it back to the Mo.

Three years later my frequent fishing partner, Josh Feigenbaum, and I stopped in the tiny, but very trouty, hamlet of Craig, Montana. As an angler I cannot think of a more perfect town. It has two bars and restaurants, one breakfast joint, two fly shops, and forty-two full-time residents. No newspaper, no museum, no professional sports team; nothing but fly-rodders and trout.

Our guide, Joe Cummings, met us for breakfast at 7:00 A.M. By that time clouds of Trico spinners

were already gyrating in the final hour of their mating dance. The mayflies began to expire after the rigors of lovemaking, and, as they did so, rising trout dimpled the water, feasting on the freshly fallen food.

Almost as thickly packed as the feeding fish, guides launched their drift boats into the flow.

"Let's head downriver," Cummings suggested, "so we can get ahead of the crowd and stake out a pod."

Within a half hour, Cummings had us on the water and in position for a dozen risers. Cummings took the measure of my cast and positioned me for a forty-foot left-reach cast, cautioning, "I want you to see the fish first. There are a bunch of trout, but the best one is rising almost straight downstream."

I squinted through the slight glare until I could see the pale form of the trout that Joe had targeted, holding in the current, finning, dropping down, turning and floating up to sip a fly. The sight of the trout, unmindful of our presence, was as exciting, in its way, as watching a cheetah stalk a gazelle; in fact, any time you can watch creatures in the wild without their sensing that you are there, you have the feeling of stolen pleasure. In such circumstances you hold your breath and try not to move. Were your presence known, or even suspected, the object of your desire would disappear.

I cast, purposefully well short of the fish. I was getting the range, correcting for windage. Finally I had it. The next problem to solve was putting the right amount of slack in the line. This required an over-the-body reach cast so that the swirling currents did not drag on the fly before it reached the trout's window.

After twenty or so casts the fish rose to my fly. I set the hook with the finesse of a woodchopper. Of course I lost the fish. Josh and Joe were sympathetic though mildly derisive. I surrendered the bow to Josh. We fish together so much that words aren't necessary in such cases. I just turned and handed him the rod. Josh is what they call a "fishy guy." His casting is good but not tournament winning, nor is he an expert when it comes to flies and hatches, but he has a keen sense for where the fish are and how they want to be enticed. In a matter of minutes he hooked a nice fish. I rushed to take my turn again and, out of a pack of a dozen fish, I lost two or three more before hooking a two-pound rainbow—fat as a pumpkinseed.

It ran like crazy, and with 5X tippet, I knew I could apply some pressure but not much. When I finally brought the fish to hand, Josh commented, "Adding in all the fish you missed today, it took an hour and a half for that baby. I knew you needed to catch a fish so I sat and shut up."

I owed him one.

We moved to a productive bank. Cummings, who is powerfully built and indefatigable, kept drifting down on the same pod then rowing back upstream for another pass. In this manner we hooked a few more fish before continuing the float and switching to hopper imitations (which the fish really clobbered). We pulled off the water at 11:00 P.M., not realizing our fatigue until we laid down our rods.

Back in town, Izaac's Cafe (Craig's après-trout waterhole, named after the patron saint of fly-fishing) was hopping. Everyone in the room wore the raccoon-face tan that comes with long days on the water looking through wraparound sunglasses. One guide pounded out country blues on an acoustic guitar, while the rest of the patrons kept time, sipped beer, wolfed down burgers, and relived trout caught, not yet caught, and still waiting to be caught. Two martinis later I left the party, hit the pillow, and had just about fallen asleep when my internal DVD kicked in, replaying an endless loop of the trout that I had missed. It was a good long while before I fell asleep.

The next morning the Tricos and the fish were at it again. Joe made straight for the scene of the previous day's fishing. The trout were on the feed but they had dropped a bit downstream to quieter water. A fishable cast had to reach farther—more delicately—than yesterday's. Luck was with me. I was as on my game this morning as I had been off it the day before, landing half a dozen trout on size 20 Tricos and 6X. Though Cummings expressed dismay at the sparseness of the spinner fall, I think it may have worked in our favor. Had it been more bounteous, perhaps the trout might not have taken the fly as eagerly. In any event, who dwells on the reasons for good luck? You just savor such moments and store them up for the days when you need reason to hope.

The Midwest

THE OZARKS:
Gettin' By

———◆———

A *conservationist once told me, "For most people, the Midwest is the place between where you are going and* where you are coming from." That's their loss. There is something about the Mississippi drainage that is as grand and stirring as any landscape in America. Its people are avid fishers and hunters. For bass and pike or "northerns," as they are known to natives, you cannot do better. Its limestone geology and abundant rainfall makes for miles of great trout habitat, although the trout are all descendents of immigrants. To my way of thinking, its greatest angling gift is the fish that I once called "the son of the Middle Border" but which my editor changed to "the bass with class." I am talking, of course, of the fish about which James Alexander Henshall wrote what is unquestionably the most famous line in American angling literature: "I consider him, inch for inch and pound for pound, the gamest fish that swims"—the smallmouth bass.

Al Agnew is the best smallmouth fisherman I ever met. By his own reckoning, this native Ozark wildlife artist has floated and fished 8,000 miles of water almost exclusively in Missouri and Arkansas. As smallmouth water goes, there is none better than the streams of the Ozarks, nor could there be. In a way, the smallmouth was designed to fit the streams of Missouri, Tennessee, Arkansas, and Kentucky, because it was there that the present strains evolved during the last ice age. When the glaciers covered the plains and shrank the Mississippi, the smallmouth retreated into the mountain streams of the upper South, and the fish adapted to fit its environment.

Good current, cool water, abundant crayfish, high clay and limestone banks, fallen trees, and plenty of rocks—from gravel to boulder size—this is the definition of good smallmouth habitat. It is also a description of the Ozark streams. Nature is indeed marvelous, but she is also logical and has tailored the smallmouth to its surroundings. The fish fits into roughly the same niche that the rainbow trout fills west of the Rockies and the brookie occupies east of the Alleghenies. The smallmouth is a large, fast, stream-borne predator who fights like the devil.

For the most part, Ozarks rivers are relatively gentle, with just enough current to move you along, but without the rapids and fast water that can spell disaster. You float down them at fishing speed, correcting your course now and then with a one-handed stroke of the paddle. You cast under the boughs. You cast to the clay banks. You cast to the half-submerged deadfalls that the locals call "root-wads." You peer down in the water at the hog suckers and the huge gar fish with their long bills. When the fishing slows down, you can easily lose yourself in the beauty of the bluffs that cup the outside of every bend, like 100-foot layer cakes of limestone and flint, laced with blue-red mineral stains and garlanded with trailing vines. The Grand Canyon is deeper and the Rockies are higher, but in their way the Ozark Bluffs are a wonder all their own.

The bluffs, or at least the limestone in them, are the key to the fishing in these waters. Here and there some granite has worked its way up to form the peaks of the hills that are known to natives as "shut ins." The most common rock, though, is water-soluble limestone. Water can seep in, freeze, and expand, opening cracks in the stone. The process also releases acids that carve huge subterranean chambers exactly like the caves where Tom Sawyer and Becky Thatcher lost their way. When the forces of erosion expose these water-filled chambers, the result is a spring. And I am not talking about pleasant little upwellings. Some of these springs are among the biggest in the world, pumping out more than 100 million gallons a day. The water runs constant and cool, at a temperature just right for smallmouths. The limestone enriches the water, producing all the food a smallmouth could ever eat. Prime conditions.

I visited Agnew at his home in the town of St. Genevieve, where, on my stroll down the main street to the Mississippi, I felt like I had been taken back in time some seventy or eighty years. The old gas station was of the vintage when service stations were white, oil company signs were circular, and gas pumps were sheltered under a peaked roof. Next door, piano music, with a spirited but erratic left hand, poured out of an open door—the unmistakable sound of a dance class. I looked inside, and sure enough, there was a group of kids: giggly girls and ill-at-ease young boys. Because there were more damsels than squires, some of the dancing couples were all girls. Farther down the street a plaque on a building told how John Audubon had once owned a mill on that site. His business failed, which was unfortunate for him, but which resulted in the great artwork and impetus to conservation that is his legacy. I continued down the lazy late-afternoon street to the end, the Mississippi. There was no esplanade or breakwater like you would find in a riverfront city, just the end of the pavement and then the river with leafy trees all along the water's edge. Here the river was an everyday fact of life without the connotation of being the mighty waterway that drains a continent. It was just a river.

"Where are you fishing?" Al's wife, Mary, asked as we were readying to leave for the evening.

"Big Creek."

"When will you be home?"

"Dark-thirty," he answered. It took me a beat of two to figure out that he meant a half-hour after dark, which, as all of you know, is as early as any fisherman returns home no matter what he promises.

We launched Al's little boat from a gravel bar on the outside of a looping bend in Big Creek. "Fishing heats up in these parts when the redbud are in bloom and the dogwood leaves are no bigger than squirrels' ears," Al explained during the drive. "The smallmouths have just started to wake up a little and they're hungry, but they haven't started to spawn yet. Then the fishing slows down some when they start to spawn."

"How long have you been fishing smallmouths, Al?"

"Almost all my life. We used to fish a lot in the lakes when I was a kid. There were a lot of largemouths and there weren't too many bass fisherman then."

"What did people fish for?"

"Oh, goggle-eye [rock bass], sunfish, carp . . . all kinds of things. Anyway, bass fishing caught on real heavy in the '60s, and the lakes got crowded and the gear got more sophisticated and nobody was fishing smallmouths in the streams very much,

so I just started floating them in my canoe and fishing whenever I could."

After casting for a half hour, I was getting few takes on my popping bug. Al suggested a rather large Lefty's Deceiver that I have used for tarpon. I humored him and tied one on. Bass, bluegill, and goggle-eyes came from everywhere. Most were just follows, but I caught two or three fish on that huge saltwater fly. And then a fine two-pound smallmouth.

As promised, we were home just after nightfall, in time to watch the St. Louis Cardinals. Mary, the kids, and the father-in-law rooted with gusto. The cards were playing the Mets, and I did little to conceal my sentiments as they beat up on the Redbirds.

Our next day's angling was on the Meramec. On weekends this forever wild river is bank full with canoes, which are at once the bane and the salvation of the Ozark waters. Canoeists like the rivers the way they are, and they have fought to preserve them. On the other side of the coin, their numbers mean you can plain forget about weekend fishing. On the other, other hand, canoeists don't fish all that much, and they keep other fishermen away and fishing pressure down. So, in a backward kind of way their presence has preserved an A-1 fishing resource.

Al is a congenitally optimistic fisherman. As far as he's concerned, every root wad holds an eleven-pounder. So we floated and we fished. We had follows. We spooked some big ones. We spooked some small ones. We kept pushing a heron downstream. Turtles, one for every piece of sunny bank, plopped into the water as we approached. We changed lures. We changed flies. We pulled onto a gravel bar and lunched on country ham, Coca-Cola, and Snickers

bars. Then we fished some more . . . on automatic pilot. Cast and retrieve, cast and retrieve. Keep your concentration. Bear down. Don't get distracted. I felt good. No false casts. I sent out a long cast, gave two gurgling pops to my bass bug, and a three-pound smallmouth smashed it. The fish jumped once, just like a tarpon. Then, just like a tarpon, it was off. It was my fault. I was so bewitched by casting, I had lost concentration, and it cost me a fish.

Ten minutes passed. I heard Al laugh behind me. Nothing very special, it was more or less the same laugh he reserved for bluegills and goggle-eyes. But the splash told me something, and I turned to see Al with one hand paddling through the fast water. His rod was bent and at the other end of the line was a big, angry, tail-walking, head-shaking bronzeback.

I grabbed a paddle and took over the navigation. Al bore down on the smallmouth. It shook its head and tried to sound. It broke water again, and the sunlight gathered in the spray of drops to form a halo that shone brilliantly and made the scales of the fish into a suit of shiny armor. We pulled to the shore and admired it: twenty inches and well over four pounds.

We were off the water in time to drive to Jackson Hollow (pronounced Jackson Holler), where I met Gene Jackson, born and raised in the hollow, leaving it only for World War II. Like the famous Sergeant Alvin York before him, Gene was a country boy with a dead eye. The army made him a sniper, and he personally dispatched many of Tojo's best before stopping a bullet himself. Joining him was his dad, another veteran who had left the hollow for World War I where he had wreaked similar havoc on the Kaiser's troops. At age ninety-four the toothless old man bested me in an arm wrestle and rewarded himself with a cold one from the cooler.

In the heyday of the guided float trip, they said, four or five johnboats would set off in caravan. This all-American sporting craft evolved, like the smallmouth, on the Ozark rivers. While the paying sports fished, a supply boat or two went ahead to the evening's campsite. When the fishing party arrived at the campsite, the tents were set up, the fire stoked. Fried fillet of black bass was, of course, a favorite item. And there was drinking and card playing and singing and the spinning of tales round the campfire.

The days of the river guide are gone now. For the most part the canoe has replaced the johnboat. And with new highways, RVs, canoe shuttles, and freeze-dried everything, today's do-it-yourself sportsman can make do without the old-time guides. But like the Jacksons, there are still those in the Ozarks who keep the old-time ways and who hunt, fish, trap, log, and do whatever it takes to enjoy their freedom and the virtue of which Ozark natives are proudest—getting by.

MINNESOTA SPRING CREEK:
It Must Be Someone's Home Pool

———◆———

*T*he biggest stream trout I ever saw was in a mid-sized creek that I never heard of. It is one of a number of splendid, clear-flowing spring creeks and freestone tributaries of the Upper Mississippi: Trout Run and Whitewater Creek, Castle Rock Creek, the mysterious-sounding Timber Coulee, the Rush and KinicKinnic, and Doc Smith Branch—whose name conjures up a kindly country medico always ready to make a house call in his trusty Model A.

These are gorgeous streams in a beautiful part of the country, especially in the spring when the first wildflowers stand out against the rich black earth, freshly plowed in long rows that flow around red barns and silos and trim white homesteads. Bob White, an artist and guide that I had met in Argentina, invited Josh Feigenbaum and me to fish there. Bob is a good fishing companion, and I jumped at the chance for him to show me his home creeks.

Food and protection are the trout's main requirements in a home. Both exist in abundance in these fertile streams. They run through farm country that seems to roll past the end of the sky, dotted with small towns where everyone gathers at the local café for endless cups of coffee. Case in point, Del's Café in the small burg of St. Charles, Minnesota. By 9 A.M. the farm chores are done and pickups are lined up outside. The counters are filled with customers in checkered shirts. Waistlines are no doubt amplified by trencherman servings of thin-sliced and crispy "American Fries." It's one of those places you come back to because after just one visit, the waitress remembers who likes decaf and how many sugars you want and how many eggs you can eat and whether you want the yolks runny or not.

St. Charles doesn't look like anyone's idea of Trout Mecca. But hold on. If you drive south, past field after freshly plowed field, you will come over a rise, and you will descend into a valley. You will pass through the shadow of limestone-cake bluffs and cross a bridge, where you will see a stream, and wildflowers in bright clumps all around, and perhaps a beaver pushing across the flow.

Winding, sandy-bottomed Whitewater Creek is long enough to get off a good cast, but not big enough for two anglers to share a pool, so we hopscotched up the stream. I'm a water-coverer. I like to walk until I see something happening and then cast to it. If nothing is happening, I'll continue upstream and with a nymph cast into likely water. Still, if there is nothing happening, I will turn around and quarter-cast down with a skittering caddis, or more often, with an all-purpose nymph. That technique is not supposed to work on clear smallish streams. But often it does for me. On that day it didn't.

I dropped back down and looked in on Bob. He crouched low to keep out of a feeding trout's window and, as he did so, he threw a tight loop under an overhanging branch. I had tried a similar tactic when I passed that tree earlier and found no takers. But Bob is a lefty, and lefties, I have observed, often have an advantage on difficult lies. They can present the fly in a way that the trout hasn't seen a thousand times. An easy-does-it cast—soft and floating, like a breakaway lay-up—brought a trout to Bob's caddis. He was fishing 6X tippet, but nonetheless he pulled back hard and bent the rod strongly. It was that or lose the fish in the brush tangle. Bob brought him to hand. Fourteen inches with the big, yellow-bordered red spots of a healthy brown.

Bob's wife Janice drove down to meet us with some much needed sandwiches, which were served by their smiling four-year-old daughter, Jesse. While we ate, Jesse practiced casting with Bob's fly rod. It was a beautiful picture, perfect—the little blond girl, the long rod, the late-afternoon light. I'd like to report that young Jesse caught a fish, but she didn't. Still, we encouraged her, and she actually looked like she could handle a rod.

Next day, Trout Run Creek was on the agenda. We stopped in the small town of Altura for snacks and cold drinks and—in deference to Minnesota's Nordic heritage—homemade pickled herring. Trout Run runs through dairy land "So green," Bob said, "it makes your eyes hurt." Upstream of our parking spot, a high bank and a grove of trees protected a long pool that I'd bet is somebody's home pool. If I were a native, it would have been mine. Shaded and perfectly shaped with lots of cover and hundreds of trout, none of them big, but so many of them in view.

I left Bob and Josh to work the pool. A gnarled old shade tree guarded the head of the pool, with big roots running into the undercut, the kind of place where bigger trout hold. I passed it by, though; it looked like a difficult lie. I walked upstream and knelt just behind a weed bed. A backhand stroke gave me room for a backcast and, with an upstream mend, it also gave me a reasonable float over two feeding fish. One rose to my caddis emerger, dead drift. With the confidence that comes from having interested a trout, I turned downstream and sent a roll cast back into the root tangle at the base of the bridge tree I had passed up. The current swept under the root, guided there by a midstream weed bed. I knew my cast would take a fish. Sure enough, the little Pheasant Tail Nymph stopped, and I felt the pounding of a fish. I brought him around the weeds and reared back on the butt of my rod. He was a nice brown. As I released him, I heard the persistent drumming of a grouse. Absentmindedly, my gaze came to rest on an old Dodge Power Wagon that lay rusty and abandoned in the field above me, a memento of the days of dependable machinery that lasted for years.

"Nice fish," a voice said, waking me from my meditation. I looked up at a middle-aged man who had materialized on the bank while I was occupied with the trout. He and his son, both spin fishermen, congratulated me, adding that they started the day with a successful turkey hunt. Father and son still had some eyeblack around their eyes, giving them a look not unlike the Beagle Boys in a Donald Duck cartoon. I congratulated them, eliciting a thorough, second-by-second account of the last earthly moments of a nineteen-pound bird.

They had been upstream and reported that a very big fish was feeding on flies in the shallows under the bluffs. It was unapproachable with their hardware, but possible with flies, they reasoned. They pointed out a shortcut that ran across the fields and back down the stream along the route of a power line.

I thanked them and waited for Bob and Josh.

We walked to the pool—the earth was freshly turned and the air was strong with the smell of manure, the sound of lowing cows, and the continuing drumbeats of the grouse. A limestone bluff towered over the stream. A deep cave bore witness to the high floods of ten thousand Aprils.

Two grassy riffles bookended the pool. Flies hatched above and below it. Only one of us could fish it. Josh drew the short straw. He waded into the riffle and waited. We saw the rise form. Josh cast well short of the target. The fish continued to feed. Josh inched closer, ever so carefully, but not quite carefully enough. The glassy tailwater shook and a very large trout sent up a big wave as it started from the shallows. The fish bucked its way against the flow. We saw its dorsal fin and tail. It looked as big as a Brittany Spaniel doggy paddling across a pool.

"Wow," seemed the most appropriate comment. We took turns guessing its weight, which is a natural response in such situations. I didn't see it for too long, but it was enormous and, sadly, gone for good. We consoled ourselves with some very cold Leinenkugel's Bock beer, just what the situation called for along with the homemade herring, which was tart and sweet and salty all at once. I lay down on the grass and listened to the plish and plash of feeding fish before dozing off.

LORDS OF THE FLY:
The Judge

———— ◆ ————

In 1952 a woman was murdered in Michigan. The subsequent trial of her murderer resulted in the book Anatomy of a Murder by the presiding judge, John Voelker, writing under the pen name of Robert Traver. It topped the best-seller list and was made into a successful movie. The director, Otto Preminger, gave Voelker a million dollars for the movie rights. That's a million 1959 dollars.

At that point, Voelker did what so few of us ever do, or ever would do. He said, "enough." Freed from the necessity of having to earn a living, he knew what he wanted to do: fish every day for wild brook trout and finish each afternoon with a round of pinochle, salty jokes, and stiff old-fashioneds.

He began to write so well about angling for trout that every fisherman who has ever cast a fly on the water can read his words and say, "Someone has found his way into my heart and written exactly what I feel." Listen to his words from "Testament of a Fisherman." (Do yourself a favor and read them aloud.)

"I fish because I love to: because I love the environs where trout are found, which are invariably beautiful, and hate the environs where crowds of people are found, which are invariably ugly; because of all the television commercials, cocktail parties and assorted social posturing I thus escape: because in a world where most men seem to spend their lives doing things they hate, my fishing is at once an endless source of delight and an act of small rebellion."

Because of his skill at getting to the heart of the fly-fishing matter, John was in his later years beset by angling pilgrims eager to sit at the feet of a venerated wise man.

This was not the John Voelker I knew. He was, at best, a reluctant saint. He was a good fisherman, but not what you would call one of the greats. His water did not offer the chance for him to prove himself with trophy fish. Mostly it contained little brookies. As fishermen are, he was sometimes overserved at cocktail hour. He was cantankerous, opinionated, generous, philosophical; in short, he was an American original—a rhapsodizer of the wild things in his own backyard.

I was in Pontiac doing a story for *Field & Stream* about Daredevle lures: killer devices but not part of the fly-rodder's arsenal. I decided to make it an all-Michigan trip and drive up to Voelker's cabin near Marquette. I found out that this made as much sense as saying, "As long as I am in New York, I might as well drive up to New Hampshire."

Five hundred miles later I arrived in the flatlands of the Upper Peninsula, or as it is locally known, the U.P. The countryside—boggy, with lots of berry tangles, birches, pines, and aspen—looks just like Finland or northern Russia. A mile or two from the highway, the road made a sharp turn. The way was pockmarked with boulders and deep ruts. Partly out of malice, but mostly out of

mischief, Voelker had festooned the gnarly deadfalls along the road with punctured mufflers, bent tail pipes, and perforated oil pans.

What I found at the end of the road was not nearly so fearsome. It was only John: gray of hair, khaki of clothes, and slightly pot of belly. He sat by a picnic table next to his cabin. It was a sweltering

July day, hot as a sauna. I had been advised to bring some bourbon as a gift. I bought the best I could find (Jack Daniel's). He took it from me, regarded it, and delivered his verdict.

"Too damned expensive," he said. "I like cheap bourbon for my old-fashioned."

We spent a short while in a getting-to-know-you conversation. The weather seemed a safe topic. We agreed that it was hot, that normally it doesn't get so hot, that it was probably hotter in Detroit, and, of course, that fishing had been quite good until the current hot spell. We came to a consensus that only a fool would fish on such a day. Then we went fishing.

John led me over a bridge that connected his two beaver ponds. A street sign (there were no streets for miles) said "Chipmunk Crossing," and sure enough a few of those perpetually panicked rodents darted across it. The path descended through the drier parts of a dense berry bog. Here and there John had placed some planks over the worst of the muck. When we came to a small dock, he pointed to the water, which was his way of saying "fish here." Then he seated himself on an old milk crate, cleared his throat, harrumphed thunderously, and set up a train of puffs from a strong Italian cigar. Between the noises and the smoke, he brought to mind an old, well-made tugboat idling.

I cast one of John's flies, a chewed up soft-hackled Pheasant Tail ribbed with copper wire: a perfect brookie fly. Sure enough a brookie took it. Then another and another. I hooked into one that felt big, but it gave two tugs and was off without affording me a glance. More than once my backcast hung up in the berry bushes, which made for a painful and prickly retrieval. The day was hot, hot, hot. Clouds of stinging deerflies and mosquitoes swarmed around me. Why hadn't I asked for one of John's Sicilian stogies?

What John really liked about fishing in his last years was hanging out with his buddies, Ted Bogden and Jim Washinawatok, who was a Menominee and the father of Native American civil-rights activist Ingrid Washinawatok, who was later murdered in Nicaragua. Pinochle, cribbage, cigars, drinks, and stories were the order of the day at the fishing camp. The group gathered each day in a little cabin with a bed, a chair, a chaste pinup, and next to it a winning pinochle hand from 1958 that was fanned out and thumbtacked to the wall. John's gang reminded me of tailgaters at NFL games who spend the whole afternoon enjoying the camaraderie and food of the parking lot without ever going inside the stadium. The Voelker group believed, as I do, that there's a lot to the allure of fishing, apart from the fish.

"We love it here," John said.

"Why do you love it John?"

"The fishing, the friends, the chipmunks, the wildflowers . . ."

"But John, surely you could get a lot better fishing somewhere else."

"I don't know. There's something about these little brook trout."

"How do you mean?"

He didn't really answer. Certain things give pleasure. That's all you really need to know. John finished his cocktail.

"I have to go home and visit my wife," he said. "I believe I am still married."

"Do you want to fish some of the rivers tomorrow?" I asked.

"I don't know," he said with a hint of a sigh. "It's awfully hot and I'm not mad at them anymore."

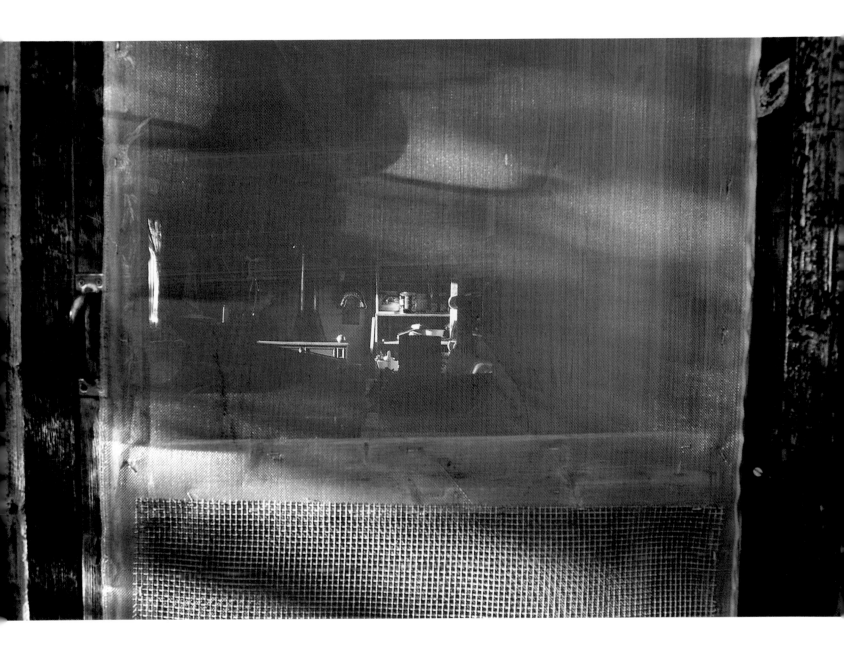

DOOR COUNTY FISH BOIL

———◆———

*D*oor *County is a very long and thin peninsula that sticks out into Lake Michigan just above Green Bay,* Wisconsin. Generations of commercial fisherman have made their living hauling their catch out of the rich lake waters. I first came across the Door County fish boil while fishing for the gargantuan brown trout of Lake Michigan. We belly boated out to pods of alewive herring that the 20-pound browns had penned up like bluefish feeding on rainbait. Biggest trout I ever saw, and I never hooked one. Grr! This recipe, which I have modified for the home cook, originated in a shore dinner that the fishing boat captains used to make for their crews and families. The original recipe calls for twenty pounds of potatoes and twenty pounds of lake trout, but the lamprey eels that made their way into the lake a half a century ago did such a good job of decimating the lakers that nowadays pretty much everyone makes this dish with whitefish chunks. Also, the original fish boil takes place outside over a really big fire. The last step in this recipe calls for the cook to throw the contents of a number-ten can filled with gasoline onto the fire. This produces a super-hot fireball, and the water in the kettle boils over, taking any fish oils or dirt with it. My advice to you is, don't throw gasoline on your indoor range.

Serves 4

Fish Boil

1½ pounds medium red potatoes
8 small onions, stem ends intact
2 quarts water
2 tablespoons kosher salt
8 ¼-pound firm-fleshed fish steaks
(such as lake trout, salmon, or
striped bass)
Freshly ground black pepper to taste
2 tablespoons flat-leaf parsley
1 lemon, cut into wedges
Melted butter for serving

Place the potatoes and onions in a stockpot, add the water and salt, and bring to a boil over high heat.

Reduce the heat to medium-high, partially cover the stockpot, and cook until the potatoes are almost tender, about 15 minutes.

Using tongs, place the fish steaks on top of the vegetables. Partially cover the pot again.

Lower the heat to medium and cook the fish for about 10 minutes, until it flakes with a fork.

Using a slotted spoon, transfer the fish to a warm platter and place the onions and potatoes alongside.

Add cracked black pepper to taste and garnish with the parsley and lemon wedges.

Serve with melted butter on the side.

BLT
(Bass, Lettuce, and Tomato)

———◆———

About fifteen years ago I visited the beautiful old town of Olney, Illinois, where my wife's side of the family has lived for a hundred and fifty years. It is straight out of *The Music Man*: big houses on shady streets lined with basswood trees, front porches on every house, and a downtown where the best restaurant excels in burgers, shakes, and batter-fried mushrooms. Melinda's uncle, Herb, was a slim and fit guy who did all right for himself as a geologist in the oil business. Whenever we visited Olney he was glad to take me out bass fishing on one of the local lakes. In the hot midwestern summers we would find the bass cooling off in the shade of a lily pad. Like largemouth everywhere, when they struck a popping bug, they put on quite a show. The take was sudden and violent and the fight satisfyingly acrobatic. One day we caught and kept a half dozen fish and brought them back to Herb's house and served them batter-fried with lettuce and tomato on toasted bread slathered with mayonnaise.

Serves 4

BLT

1 cup all-purpose flour
1 teaspoon salt
1 teaspoon freshly ground black pepper
1 cup buttermilk
1 cup cornmeal
A neutral oil, such as vegetable or canola
8 bass fillets, trimmed to 4 inches in length
Toasted bread slices, mayonnaise, lettuce, and tomatoes for the sandwiches

Season the flour with the salt and pepper, and spread over a large plate.

Pour the buttermilk into a medium bowl and spread the cornmeal over another large plate.

Heat a cast-iron skillet over medium-high heat and add about an inch of oil.

Dredge the fillets in the flour.

Shake off the excess flour and dip fillets one at a time in the buttermilk, then dredge in the cornmeal.

As each fillet is ready, put it in the cast-iron pan and fry for about 2 minutes, or until flaky but moist.

Turn the fish and fry another 2 minutes, then remove from the pan and drain on paper towels.

Assemble the sandwiches with the mayonnaise, lettuce, tomato, and bass fillet.

THE SOUTHEAST

DOWNTOWN BONEFISH

———◆———

If absence makes the heart grow fonder, then I am besotted with the bonefish of the Florida Keys. Of all the gamefish that one can fish for, these Floridians are the wariest. I have thrown flies at them for years and years. Getting a cast off without spooking one counts as a moral victory. Hooking one merits a glass of champagne. And catching one . . . well, that happens so rarely that I hardly know what to suggest by way of celebration. Mind you, this is not true of all bonefish. By way of comparison, the Bahamian cousins of the Keys bones are like rich country bumpkins just begging to be fleeced by a flimflam man. Still, you fish where you can when you can, so when guide Allan Finkelman and Al Caucci invited me to Islamorada for a few days, I went.

Finkelman, who has since taken a civilian job, was at that time among the elite of Keys guides, which is no mean feat for a transplanted New Yorker. Up north, he was a top commercial photographer who discovered fly-fishing. He quickly became a regular on the tournament circuit, often placing in the money. He finally threw over the New York thing, moved south to the Keys, and set himself up in the guide business. Fly-fishing, once it grabs hold of your soul, will do that to you.

On our first day, warm winds from the south brought the promise of good fishing, but they arrived with a morning blanket of fog in the back country (the Gulf side of the Keys), so Finkelman slowly made his way to the nearby and famously difficult Downtown flats of Islamorada. From Ted Williams to Lefty Kreh to A. J. McClane to Lee Wulff—every great fisherman you can name has thrown a fly at these guys. Add to that every mediocre to poor angler who comes to the Keys, and the result is educated fish who have seen absolutely everything.

As we came out of the channel that leads to Downtown, I spotted the flickering tail of a feeding bonefish in the opalescent light, wagging like a spirited puppy. We closed the distance. I cast seventy feet as delicately as if I were presenting a tiny fly to a dimpling trout.

"Perfect," Caucci said, but the bone had turned so that he couldn't see my fly. I tried another and placed it right in front of the fish, perhaps three inches from his mouth.

"Even more perfect," Finkelman encouraged. "Now don't move the fl—"

But before he could finish his sentence, I instinctively gave my fly a short strip. That subtle movement was enough to startle the bone, who waked off the flat like a streaking torpedo.

"That's Downtown fishing," Allan consoled. "Anything funny looking and they're out of here."

The fog lifted, so we headed into the back country to try our luck. Fishing the drop-off of Nine Mile Flat, we put three sea trout in the live well, then landed and released a Spanish mackerel as well as a dozen ladyfish up to four pounds . . . a wonderful mixed

bag, but not enough to hold our attention after we saw a tarpon erupt in the distance.

"The tarpon could have come in from the Gulf with the warming water," Finkelman reasoned, as he poled Caucci into position. Caucci's casting style is unmistakable, a closed stance with an over-the-top motion and a sweet-looking long and narrow loop.

Caucci worked his twelve-weight tarpon rod, placing the fly in front of the fish. Four casts failed to rouse it. The wind turned north and, as if a switch had been thrown, the tarpon stopped rolling.

That night we gathered to strategize over a bottle of Puligny Montrachet (Finkelman is a major wine lover). I prepared the trout with a light coating of super crisp panko crumbs and a sauce of grapefruit, shallots, sugar, lemon juice, and cayenne. Fresh fish and grapefruit in season . . . hard to beat.

A cold front pushed through the next morning, causing the bones to retreat from their already tentative forays onto the flats. But a run up to Biscayne Bay finally brought us upon a pod of tailers in the late afternoon. I took two unrewarded shots before Caucci connected. A nine-and-a-half-pound bone jerked his rod. Al's response suggested a man with a high-speed dowsing rod. "Couch," as he has been called since childhood, broke into the smile of the just and victorious; it had been three years since he last took a January bonefish in Florida.

My big chance came on our last day. The weather forecast called for a warm surge and light southern winds—a perfect combo for summoning tarpon. But, as it had two days ago, a thick fog bank kept us from running for two hours. Bummer!

During our down time, Finkelman worked on my cast.

"Everyone, especially the trout fisherman, tries to muscle the cast in order to get up line speed. It's true you need a long cast, but it is also true that it takes surprisingly little physical power to launch one."

He demonstrated, taking up a rod. "I strip off sixty feet of line and then cast it as lightly as I can. If the line slaps against the reel you have excess power. So lighten up even more until finally the cast dies. If you correct that last cast with just a little more power, you are now in the zone."

As directed, I cast long and slow, without much effort. By adding a double haul I reached out ninety feet with no histrionic contortions. Ever since that day, whenever I find myself overcasting to maintain my line speed, I summon up the image of Allan in the bow of his boat, launching a cast. Slowly, almost maddeningly so, he let the backcast unfurl and then, like a breeze changing direction almost imperceptibly, he moved into the forward cast. When done correctly, you can be standing on a flats boat in dead calm water, yet your casting motion won't rock the boat a bit.

But the purpose of casting is catching fish, and the purpose of guiding is to find them. We ran to hell and back looking for fish. An unpredicted north wind scotched our tarpon plan. A forty-minute dash across Florida Bay to Flamingo might have given us a shot at tailing redfish, but the redfish were God knows where.

Finally, with very little time to spare if I was to make my plane, we ran for home. Wouldn't you know it? About two hundred yards from the dock, back at Downtown, Allan brought the boat abruptly off plane. "We just ran over forty tarpon. They are all over the flat."

This was my chance! I took at least twenty shots at tarpon. My casts, long and true, either spooked them into riotous commotion or, worse, went unnoticed. Whatever. It set my heart thumping, gave me thrill after thrill and in the end confirmed, once again, that I am still a Not Quite Ready for Downtown Player. This makes me a member of a big club.

TARPON IN THE MARQUESAS

———————

There is a tide in the affairs of men, Brutus confided to Cassius in Shakespeare's Julius Caesar. *He goes on to say that it must be taken at the flood*—the clear import of the message being if you miss the peak, you may miss it all. Thus the fateful call that came from Allan Finkelman early one June spurred me to run to the Florida Keys. It went something like, "Peter, I just had a cancellation. I think you should get down here. Yesterday I had an absolute beginner out. The guy could maybe get out twenty feet of line. He caught six tarpon."

I had never caught six tarpon: neither on one day nor in my whole life. Tarpon are, in a sense, the peak of the fly-fishing game. They must be approached with the caution reserved for dimpling trout, yet the cast to them must be as powerful as a toss into the fifty-mile-an-hour winds of Tierra del Fuego. The hookset requires a huge sweeping motion, and the fight is one of nonstop brute force. Moreover both the angler and the target are usually moving. Think 3-D chess and rugby rolled into one.

From the time I left my house in Brooklyn, during the whole cab ride out to Kennedy, then all through the flight to Miami and the drive to the Keys, I replayed the same scene: me, Allan, and a large tarpon, at least a hundred pounds. Allan swings the boat for a shot at an incoming pod—six dark shapes moving like a wolf pack across the copper green waters. I hold my fire. The shapes move closer until they are big as a man. I cast. One fish turns. His mouth opens wide as he takes the fly. I strip-strike with a long stroke and drive the hook home like an assassin sinking his dagger. The fight is on.

Optimistically, my concern was whether I would be strong enough to subdue six tarpon in a day. Or, as seemed more likely, since Finkelman's angler of the day before was a true duffer, would I have the strength to best eight tarpon . . .

Of such thoughts are great disappointments made. No sooner had I pulled into Allan's carport than he came downstairs to greet me with the words, "You're not going to believe this."

When it comes to anticipating bad news, I always believe it. "Not going to believe what, Allan?"

"I spoke to my friend in Tavernier [a short ways up the Keys from Islamorada] and he said he had just seen the most amazing thing. For hours and hours all he could see was tarpon, maybe three hundred thousand of them, all headed north."

"You mean, like it's over? Like every tarpon in the Upper Keys has headed back north?"

"Well, maybe not. I mean, it couldn't be."

But it was thus. In three days of looking, in every cut where the big ones are known to lay up, in the back country and out front, all the way over to the Glades, there was not a tarpon to be found. Sometimes I think I would prefer a guide to tell me, just before I leave on a trip, that the fishing really sucks. That way I would have a fighting chance of my luck making a right turn into good fortune instead of a left into futility. And

I'm not knocking guides here. It's just a beef that I have with Lady Luck.

On the other hand, and just as surprisingly, there are those days when you hit it right: the weather is fine, the tide is right, the wind is behind you, and the fish are everywhere.

It was at such a time that I caught my first tarpon out in the Marquesas—a lovely string of islets about an hour's boat ride from Key West.

Melinda and I jumped at an invitation from John Cole to stay with him at his short-lived but wonderful Key West Angler's Club. Cole, a New York native, spent twenty years as a commercial fisherman on Long Island's East End. From there he went to Maine, where he founded the *Maine Times*, wrote regularly for the *Boston Globe*, and authored a number of books, including the exquisitely lyrical *Striper*. In 1986, a visit to the Keys began what he calls "the obsession of my later years": the pursuit of tarpon, chronicled in spare heartfelt prose in *Tarpon Quest*.

Fishing for tarpon with the author of the book was an offer I couldn't imagine turning down, so we drove straight through from Delray to Key West.

Over cocktails and stone crabs, John, his wife Gloria, Melinda, and I passed an extended happy hour cum dinner. Cole had set us up for a 5 A.M. rendezvous with a local guide, David Kesar, so we turned in early,

but I was too excited to sleep. At 4:15 A.M. I rolled out
of bed, lumbered into the kitchen, cut an orange, put
it on the juicer, and squeezed fresh juice. Soon I felt
something cold and wet running over my toes. I had
forgotten to put a glass under the juicer. Eventually,
though, I got on track, and we grabbed a quick breakfast. John slept in. He would join us in the evening.

Still in darkness, Kesar idled out of the harbor
before heading full throttle toward the Marquesas.
We arrived at daybreak, just as a porpoise leaped
across our path, catching the first rays of the sun.

In front of us, plainly visible on the white flat, a
pod of tarpon rolled. They were big enough to get
all of my attention. I felt myself shaking as we
approached them, but my cast was adequate, leading
the tarpon by a few yards. I stripped my fly. I saw a
huge flash of silver. The tarpon had eaten my fly!

"Strip until you come tight," Kesar ordered. I
felt the line go taut. "Strike as hard as you can," he
continued. I hit the fish. "Again," he commanded.

I hit him again, really hard. My line rose as the
tarpon rocketed from the water six feet in the air. I
lowered the rod, bowing to the king as the saying goes,
so that my sixteen-pound leader did not have to bear
the full force of eighty pounds of fish in free fall.

Cole had told me, "You have to dominate the fish,"
and I tried to do that, leaning back on the rod, pumping the fish, responding to his 100-yard runs and
thrashing leaps. Kesar timed the fight on a stopwatch.
At 37 minutes 54 seconds, the tarpon stopped. We
saw a foamy commotion up ahead. A big mouth came
out of the shallow water. Shark! I saw the snout break
water, and the jaws closed on my fish. It gave two
furious slaps with its tail, and then my line went slack.

And that was the end of that. The sun beat down on the flats. The tarpon left, and we returned to the club. I slept until 1:30 P.M., then we went to town for some lunch.

Melinda, relishing the rare freedom of having no children around, decided to forgo the evening fishing and to stay behind on the veranda for a couple of hours of uninterrupted reading.

John and I went down to the dock where Kesar waited. We were going to fish close in. The worm hatch was on.

In early summer, at the height of the tarpon run, a small red worm—the palolo—hatches out of the coral, sucked into the tidal currents where the tarpon hang, gorging themselves.

We moved to the head of the harbor. The ebb tide poured out at a strong clip. I looked down and saw a little squiggle in the water—palolo, millions of them. The tarpon started to feed; the surface of the water looked like a trout pool in a mayfly hatch, except these were 100-pound tarpon—acres of them—leaping and crashing.

With so much food on the water, the tarpon were selective. I cast and cast. The tarpon weren't interested. I heard the pesky grumble of a jet skier and turned my head to see if they were bearing down on me. That was one tarpon's cue to hit. My reel zinged, and the fish broke me off.

"Hmm," Cole observed with what passes for loquaciousness in a Down Easter. "That fish hit when the fly was hanging in the current. I think maybe we should treat this tarpon like salmon in the stream."

Just like a New Brunswick salmon fisherman, Cole cast across the current and let the fly swing in the flow. He twitched the rod and suggested, "Take, take," to the tarpon as portentously as Babe Ruth was said to have called his shot in Wrigley Field.

The tarpon responded. As the fish leaped, I thought of the first time I'd been to a drive-in movie. I remember Clark Gable's head on the screen, a hundred times larger than any head I had ever seen: it was about the same relationship the tarpon bore to my biggest trout.

The tarpon fell back to the water with the crash of a tree falling in the forest. And then he was gone. The hatch was over. The sky darkened and a waterspout moved toward us, its funnel cloud tightening. We upped anchor and raced away from the sinuous spiral bearing down on us. It looked like a black snake with an evil yellow aura. Here and there a rolling tarpon disturbed the fast-darkening water.

SHARKS

———◆———

I *suppose you could call shark fishing the NASCAR version of fly-rodding, or perhaps the WWF. It is* elemental, huge, violent, and nuts. I tried it for the first and only time at the invitation of Tim Borski, who is an artist both at the tying vise and with palette and brush.

Although sharks will occasionally take a fly presented without the inducement of live bait, one's chances of hooking up improve when a chum slick is thrown into the mix. Borski's preferred bait is freshly caught barracuda: the pungent oil of the barracuda is a powerful attractant even at long distances.

Somewhere between Key Largo and Islamorada, we fished for bait on a productive reef where we quickly took eight small barracuda on spinning tackle and lures. With our bait wells filled, we motored over a gently rocking sea toward a huge flat that shimmered like green jade in firelight.

Borski set up a drift on one edge of the flat, ceding the prime spot to Allan Finkelman and I, about a mile to the east. By working two edges, he reasoned, we would drive prey between us, and where the prey went, the sharks would follow.

Allan butterflied a 'cuda. He passed a rope through its gills and tied it off on the bow cleat. It made for nice pungent chum.

We waited.

"You got one at 5:30 about two hundred yards out," Allan said.

I turned my head and picked up a silhouette moving into the tide with the shoulder-

shrugging motion of a shark on the prowl. And then, like a dog responding to his master's whistle, he turned, straight for the boat. No question about it, he had picked up the scent.

"Hold your cast," Allan said. "Remember he can't see that well. Get the fly right in front of his eyes when he is thirty feet out."

When the shark came into range I heaved the huge fly. The shark swam right by.

"You stripped too much. Keep it still or just barely move it so that it stays next to his eye."

The sharks kept coming and I kept presenting bait. They looked interested. Finally one locked onto my fly and I saw his mouth open. He's got it!" Allan said.

But I was too slow. "You have to come tight and strike hard," Allan explained.

Just then Borski called Allan on the phone. It was like listening to a Bob Newhart routine, where you hear only one end of the conversation but, still, you can figure out exactly what is being said on the other end.

"You've got three in the slick . . . He's got it! You dropped him? The other one turned off. The third one's turning?" Then, speaking, "Tim's got one, let's go."

We approached to within fifty yards of Borski's boat (leaving the shark plenty of running room). For the next ten minutes, Borski repeated the same tiring motion. He reeled, reached one hand forward on the rod, and then brought his shoulders into the effort as he backed up and lifted. We got our first look at his fish—a tawny, yellowish lemon shark about eight feet long. After another ten minutes of

lifting and chasing, Borski brought it to the boat. We snapped pictures, and Borski released it.

"We've got a ton of bait out, and we were on a good spot. Hop over on our boat," Borski offered, and I accepted.

Borski and fellow guide Jon Milchman strung out all five barracudas and shook them vigorously to release scent. I placed my fly in the water about ten feet from the bait ball. This would be more like dapping than fly-fishing, but distinctions of angling nomenclature mattered very little when a huge lemon rocketed out of a cloud of mud as it turned on the fly.

Buck fever, or its shark equivalent, overtook me and I snatched the fly away. I barely had time to collect my thoughts as another shark bore down and inhaled the fly. It pulled my rod as violently as anything I have ever had on the line, and that includes blue marlin. We followed the fish, and I reeled for dear life, pumping to recover line whenever I could. At last I caught sight of what I took to be a two-hundred-pound fish.

"About a hundred and twenty," Milchman said, which would have made it as big as any tarpon I've hooked. Remembering how Tim had fought his shark, I backed up and lifted, attempting to bring the fish alongside the boat, but on the third try, he broke free.

That night I called my family and told them about my 150-pound shark (and in my mind, by that time, he was). Next day when I returned a friend's phone call, he congratulated me: "I heard you caught a three-hundred-pound shark!" And thus are fish tales spun.

MEALS:
A Speckled Trout Dinner

———◆———

*N*owhere is the gone-fishin', 1950s rhythm of the Keys felt more strongly than in the angler-friendly town of Islamorada. They like fishermen there. The motels have a very early breakfast so you can get on the water quickly, and the local market takes your sandwich order at night ("No need to pay me, I will remember your face") and it will be freshly made at 5:30 in the morning, waiting for you in a brown bag with your name on it. For dining out, I have always adored the painted cement-block restaurant called Many & Isa's, which was run by and named for a Guatemalan couple who raise their own key limes for their supernal key lime pie. The restaurant bric-a-brac included a fine picture of Ted Williams (a former Islamorada resident) flanked by a brace of large tarpon.

The chef had a light hand with fried fish, served with fried plantains and a salad. There were two sauces, both homemade, plunked down with the fish: one of green chilies and garlic, the other of tomato, mint, garlic, and chili peppers. Try them, and the words *tartar sauce* may disappear from your vocabulary.

On one visit in the late '80s I had booked a day's fishing in Florida Bay with John Guastavino, who was also the chief mixologist at the Cheeca Lodge. Although it has become a more full-service resort, back then it was an upscale fishing lodge with lots of knotty pine, iceberg lettuce with Thousand Island dressing, and a pianist who knew every song Fred Astaire and Hoagy Carmichael ever sang.

John and I met early in the morning in Tavernier and sped across Florida Bay. As we slalomed through the channel markers, a pair of dolphins leapt in front of us. Farther on an eagle took wing while an osprey lit on a piling, a healthy sea trout in its talons. As the coast came into view, Guastavino cut his engines and began to pole us along the flat.

I tied on a shrimp imitation and took up my casting position in the bow. We were at mid-tide, so the water was too deep for tailing redfish to show. Instead we looked for the puff of mud that signals a feeding stingray. Redfish like to follow just behind, picking up any food dislodged from the grass beds by the flapping of the ray's wings.

"Redfish, ten o'clock," Guastavino advised in less urgent tones than the anxiety-inducing alarm of most guides. "Fifty feet out. Forty. Moving left. Cast."

At the same moment, I saw a small tight puff much closer in. I lay my fly in the middle of the smoky emanation, pulled twice, and was fast to a strong fish. It sliced across the flat, taking line and shaking its head. A lemon shark moved across my line, but happily he noticed neither line nor fish.

"It's a trout, a really nice trout," John called down from the platform. Within five minutes I brought in a fat 22-inch speckled trout (up North, it's called a weakfish) and tossed him into the live well. No matter what happened from here on out, the day was not a loss. With the approach of a towering black cloud, the skies turned a pulsing misty green and yellow that means "really big storm on the way." We decided to

leave the reds for another day and return to port.

With the rain pelting us, John filleted the fish at the dock. I threw the fillets in a bag of ice and drove to have dinner with an old college buddy in Coconut Grove. He welcomed me with a fine single malt Scotch. My thoughts turned first to the trout and then to Many and Isa's sauce. There was no reason it

wouldn't work with fresh ingredients. The acid from the tomatoes brightened the taste. The mint snuck through as a high note, sliding on top of the heat of a couple of fresh chilies. Served alongside a plate of skillet-fried potatoes, it was a splendid tropical concoction that I have since tried on striped bass and bluefish.

Serves 6

Salsa

2 tablespoons olive oil
1 Thai (hot) chile, seeded and diced
2 garlic cloves, diced
1 shallot, diced
2 tomatoes, peeled, seeded, and chopped
¼ cup fresh mint, chopped
¼ cup white wine or lemon juice, or a mixture of both
Salt and freshly ground black pepper

To make the salsa, warm the oil in a medium frying pan over medium heat and sweat the chile for 1 minute.

Add the garlic and shallot, and sauté until the garlic turns golden, about 3 minutes.

Add the tomatoes, bring to a simmer, and simmer about 5 minutes until the tomatoes release their liquid.

Add salt and pepper to taste.

Add the mint and deglaze the pan with the wine or lemon juice. Set aside.

Fish

2 speckled trout fillets, skin removed (about 1 ½ pounds each)
2 tablespoons olive oil
2 sprigs fresh rosemary
Salt and freshly ground black pepper to taste

To make the fish, prepare a charcoal fire on a clean grill wiped down with olive oil. Dredge the fillets in olive oil and add salt and pepper and the rosemary to taste.

Grill over hot coals 2 minutes per side (you might want to use a Griffo Grill or a fish or burger holder so that the fillets don't break up and fall through the slats in the grill).

Remove the fillets to a platter, spoon the salsa over the fillets, and serve.

CAPE FEAR

———◆———

The false albacore of Harker's Island on North Carolina's Outer Banks are fast, gaudy, and pugnacious. When they show up in force from late October through December, they are anywhere from fifty to 100 percent larger than their Montauk cousins. As it is with other species—for example brown trout—there is a point where the difference in size becomes a difference in kind. Though you may have experience with the smaller members of the species, you need new angling skills to tangle with the big boys.

Unlike most fisheries—whose origin is lost in heavily embroidered legend—fly-rodding for albies at Cape Lookout is in many ways the invention of one man, retired law professor and angling author Tom Earnhardt of Raleigh, North Carolina. A lifelong freshwater fly fisherman, he first caught the occasional albie when he started fly-fishing the North Carolina coast in the 1970s, but it wasn't until the mid-1980s that he had an angling epiphany as he realized that albacore were most likely to be caught on small flies rather than the large ones he had been using to that point. He became an albacore addict. It took four or five years for word of the great fishing he had found to spread through the fly-fishing community. By the recent turn of the century, Cape Lookout had become a place of pilgrimage for the saltwater fly rodder.

There is much beside fishing to recommend a trip to this sleepy fishing village, which, despite its prime beachfront location, remains a place where a salt-pitted mobile home is still more common than a shiny new Mercedes. On the drive there you will have many opportunities to sample one of the glories of American cuisine: authentic, slow-cooked,

wood-smoked eastern Carolina barbecue. Its greatest practitioners cook whole hogs over hickory and pecan, chop the meat into a coarse mince (studded with crispy cracklings), douse it with a mix of hot pepper and vinegar, and finish with some ubiquitous and mysterious "secret seasonings."

Equally old-timey is the delightfully ramshackle Harker's Island Fishing Center. In season you may depend upon finding twenty or thirty skiffs there. Guides—with beards that range from two-day stubble to permanent fur—gather to gossip on a bench outside the door of the bait shop, sipping an early-morning Coca-Cola. At their feet, you will encounter an equally laid-back gathering of golden retrievers, black labs, and other sweet-dispositioned hounds contentedly chewing on scraps from the commercial fishing boats.

Well fed and brimming with the optimism of a man who knows a sure bet, I arrived there a few years ago in mid-November. I was surprised to see so few boats. On previous trips, the license plates on the boat trailers told the observant visitor that serious anglers from Cape Cod to Key Largo had gathered for the autumn riot at Harker's.

"I sure hope you brought a change of luck," said Rob Pasfield, a seasoned guide and heir to the fishing center's proprietor, Bob Pasfield.

"One fish all day," Pasfield lamented. His mood was seconded by the small band of sunburned guides. But still, I knew that the recent weather pattern had been stable and that the morrow would bring sun and relatively calm winds. I went to bed believing, as I always do, that the tide was running my way.

Next morning under a high blue sky, my guide, Ken Kuhner, headed his 23-foot Contender past the Hook at the end of Cape Lookout (once known as Cape Fear). About a mile out from the lighthouse, the sky was dark with diving birds.

"Bonanza," I thought out loud.

"Flounder fisherman," Kuhner corrected. "And the birds

don't mean a thing. They're gannets, probably feeding on mullet."

We continued to a rip known as the Eastern Slough. Wrecks on its treacherous shoals have contributed mightily to the reputation of the Outer Banks as the Graveyard of Ships. Right in the middle of the rip, with a fast incoming tide and three-foot seas, Ken picked up albacore on his screen. I steadied myself against the gunwale and cast into the current.

Soon I was fast to a demon of an albacore. Faster than a bonefish, he tore off two hundred yards of backing, then threw himself in reverse and bore down on us. I reeled in but could not recover line fast enough and, with the release in tension, the fish was off.

"You have to strip faster. Hand over hand, like you were fighting a trout," Kuhner advised.

I couldn't figure out exactly how to follow his instructions.

Ken explained. "Larger albacore have a big patch of soft tissue exposed when they open their jaws. The hook will make a big enough hole that the minute you slacken up, the fish is gone . . . every time."

When the next fish struck, I stripped in line with a hand-over-hand motion like a man shimmying up a tree to chop down coconuts, pausing to spank the reel for dear life.

For an honest fifteen minutes, the fish and I did our long-distance dance. Finally—and mercifully for my tired arms—the albacore, all lit up from the fight, came to the net.

With that, the tide died. The albies disappeared and we went searching. A dark shape rose from the depths, bigger and bigger. With a gush of spray and a loud puff, a breathy old whale breached twenty yards in front of us. Just as quickly, he or she went down before we could guess the species. The whale showed again, this time even more briefly. And then it was gone.

Content with three takes, one nice fish, and some wildlife up close, we retired to the Hook.

However, once we were inside its sheltering arms a pod of albacore slashed on the surface, pushing a spray of terrified baitfish into the air. I tied on a Crease fly.

I hooked up and fought a strong fish. It led me to the stern, feinted under the engine, then reversed course. Ken netted the albacore, this one slightly smaller than my first.

Seeing that something was up, the other fly-rod guides eased into the feeding fish. With that, the albacore became uncatchably boat shy.

Across the channel, a herd of wild ponies sauntered along the beach. They are the lone descendents of the once-domesticated farm animals of Diamond City, an ancient settlement that was abandoned after the San Ciriaco hurricane of 1899. The long-maned ponies nibbled on sea grass and shook their manes. They disappeared over the dune into the dying light of late autumn.

We called it a day. On the way back to the main highway I recalled a saying that Bob Pasfield, the proprietor of Harker's, had shared in explanation on the great number of churches we had noticed while driving to Harker's. "If this part of North Carolina is the Bible Belt," he recited, "then Harker's Island is its buckle." As I pulled out of the parking lot, I noticed the the old church with a black-lettered signboard. "Jesus first. Oysters second," it said.

REDFISH IN BLUESVILLE

———◆———

*I*n the way that southerners take life at a little slower—they would say more civilized—pace than Manhattanites, the redfish goes about his day less frenetically than the more in-your-face striper. Both, though, are good-sized fish who come into the skinniest water, where you may stalk and catch them on a fly. You can fly-fish for reds from the Atlantic coast of Florida, then along the Gulf all the way to Texas. I have caught these fish in the lagoons of Cape Canaveral, in the shadow, quite literally, of the *Challenger*, on the mud flats where the Everglades end, and outside Merida in the Yucatan fishing with a hand line that I learned to use from some Mayans. If I had to pick one place, though, I would say my favorite redfishing is just south of New Orleans. In much the same way that I get an extra kick out of fishing in New York City, where I can slip out of my waders and go to a concert at Carnegie Hall, I love crawling around the French Quarter of New Orleans, eating shrimp and oysters, catching Alan Toussaint's rocking piano at Tipitina's, and waking up bleary-eyed for the trip down to the wild places where pirates used to hang out and redfish still do.

On one such morning, Josh Feigenbaum and I left the French Quarter at 6:30 A.M. The die-hards were still partying. Mist swirled along the Mississippi as we made for our rendezvous with a man mountain of a guide, the soft-spoken Bubby Rodriguez. We were after redfish in the shallows south of Lafitte's Landing.

As we crossed the Mississippi bridge, the cityscape of New Orleans gave way to a sparsely populated strip of land with wood-sided houses on stilts, lush trees heavy with Spanish moss, roadside stands offering shrimp, oysters, speckled trout, and redfish, and endless businesses dedicated to the building, repairing, sale, and storage of boats. The Barataria Fire Department sported a Coca-Cola emblem on its sign.

We put in at the landing and clambered aboard Rodriguez's custom-designed "mud boat": an extremely shallow draft, narrow aluminum boat with a V prow. It was designed expressly for the trackless maze of marshes and channels that gave haven to generations of pirates and smugglers—and redfish.

Rodriguez, like most men in Louisiana, has been fishing and hunting whenever he could since he was a boy. He was not, however, a lifelong fly fisherman. He was a duck hunter. All through the season, he prowled the shallow marshes. While waiting for something to happen, which duck hunters inevitably spend a lot of their time doing, he often noticed redfish feeding in the shallow water, their tails waving in the air as they rooted for shrimp. To an angler this is seductive, breath-robbing sight. At that time no one fished these waters because they were hard to get to and the fish were considered impossibly spooky.

That's just the kind of fishing I love. Stealth and the ability to deliver an accurate cast over distance are demanded to hook up with a red in these conditions. Mere brute casting won't do it, nor will a delicate touch all by itself. You need both.

We motored along winding channels, some less than a foot deep. The only evidence of humanity was the occasional sign, put up by the oil companies, warning of buried pipelines.

As we entered a wide lagoon. Rodriguez cut the engines and poled along the flat. He asked me to cast as long a line as felt comfortable. I threw seventy feet. In this way he knew what he could and could not ask of me. He spotted a fish. I saw nothing, but cast where he told me to. A redfish boiled and took. Out of reflex, I raised my rod and the fish was off. Grrr . . . a trout strike never works on a saltwater fish.

Echoing my thoughts, Bubby said, "Strike by pulling the line, just like a tarpon. If you raise the rod you lose him every time."

As he spoke I saw something glistening and waving against the grass.

"Tailing fish," I said.

Bubby had me hold my fire until he positioned us to give me "fair wind." I liked the phrase, which was new to me. He meant he wanted to put the wind behind my casting arm.

"Go," he said.

I cast. The fish followed. Bubby told me to keep stripping. The fish took. I raised my rod again, and the fish was off. It's hard to break the trout habit.

We moved off the flat (you just get a few shots and then the fish are gone). I handed the rod to Josh. We ran through another maze of channels and Josh continued to cast for an hour with no luck. I ate a sandwich of salami and provolone on French bread and remarked on a line of trees running along a low ridge.

"We call that kind of ridge a chenier," Bubby said.

I took the rod again. My eyes had accustomed themselves to spotting redfish finning beneath the surface. In the brown-tinged water, they have a burnt-copper glow.

Seeing was a mixed blessing, however. Where before I relied on Bubby's accurate directions, I was now flying without instruments. I consistently cast

too far in front of the redfish, as if I were leading a cruising bonefish. Two such casts and the reds "had us made," according to Bubby. Rather than spooking like a bone and taking off like greased lightning, the redfish, in such situations, saunters off slowly and deliberately, with infuriating disregard for the angler.

"You have to put it right in front of their mouth," Bubby counseled. I unloosed a long cast, just in front of the redfish. He took the fly, a crab-like Wobble Spoon, which qualifies as the most rednecky fly name ever. I set the hook with my line hand. It was a terrific fight, and soon Josh obligingly netted a gorgeous eight-pound redfish that went into the cooler for that night's dinner in New Orleans. Bubby filleted the fish as quickly as I have ever seen it done. Within the hour, we were back in New Orleans for mint juleps.

REDFISH AND SWEET POTATO RAGOUT

———◆———

Susan Spicer is the chef/owner of one of New Orleans's top restaurants, Bayona. This is saying something in a city known for its cuisine, but Spicer, who was raised partly in Europe and who worked in some of the great kitchens of France, is both an inventive modern chef and a keeper of tradition. I invited her to fish one day with Bubby Rodriguez. In return she agreed to make up a recipe for our catch.

Just before dawn on the appointed morning I opened my eyes as a bolt of lightning reached down into the waters of the Gulf. Not a good sign. Boomers rolled across the red sky as Bubby pulled up to the landing.

"Sorry I'm late," Bubby said. "I had to hide from one of those thunderstorms, but I think we'll be okay for a few hours."

"Crash!" went the thunderclouds, as the bolts struck the Gulf, but Bubby swore the storms were moving around us.

We motored through winding channels and came onto a broad lagoon. Bubby pointed out the V-wakes of cruising reds. He took up his push pole and moved us on an interception course. Susan threw a buzzbait with her spinning rod. I stuck with a fly. The air was so still and the water so calm that my fly seemed to have the better chance. I saw a cherry-red fish with its back clear out of the water and sent a fairly long cast about six inches in front of his nose. The redfish turned, I stripped. He pushed a bow wave in front of him. I hit him and soon landed a six-pounder. Dinner, or in this case breakfast, was assured.

Serves 4

Sweet Potato Ragout

2 tablespoons olive oil	To make the ragout, warm the oil and butter in a large sauté pan over medium-high heat.
1 tablespoon unsalted butter	
2 peeled cooked sweet potatoes, diced	Add the sweet potatoes, half the onion, and half the chiles, and cook approximately 5 minutes, until the onions are soft and translucent, stirring the pan once.
1 Spanish onion, diced	
2 poblano chiles, diced	
2 tomatoes, peeled, seeded, and diced	Add the remaining onion and chile, and the tomatoes, thyme, and salt and pepper to taste and sauté for about 7 minutes.
1 tablespoon chopped fresh thyme	
Salt and freshly ground black pepper	Add the scallions, toss, and keep warm while you fry the fish.
2 tablespoons chopped scallions	

Fish

½ cup cornmeal	To make the fish, season the cornmeal with the salt and pepper and spread over a large plate.
½ teaspoon salt	
½ teaspoon freshly ground black pepper	Dredge the fillets in the cornmeal.
2 large skinned redfish fillets, cut in half (about 5 ounces each serving)	Heat the butter in a large skillet over medium-high heat and add enough olive oil to come ⅛ inch up the sides of the pan.
	When the fat is very hot (but not smoking), place the fillets in the pan.
	If you fold over the thin tail of the fillet so that the whole piece is of uniform thickness, you will avoid ending up with a dried-out fillet.
2 tablespoons unsalted butter	Fry for about 3 minutes on each side, until flaky but not dry.
About ¼ cup olive oil	Serve the fish with the ragout on the side.

LORDS OF THE FLY:
Jack Allen

———◆———

Jack Allen first came to Florida in a late-model 1952 Ford. One look at the Everglades, and he knew he'd found the Promised Land. Everything I know about the Glades I learned from Jack. I pick up something from everyone I fish with, but I've probably learned the most from Jack. I have learned how to handle wind, how to hit targets, the neat trick of skipping a fly beneath an overhanging branch, the importance of slowing down your cast, the hunger-curing sorcery worked by a sandwich of peanut butter, honey, and bananas, and the sufficiency of two-wheel drive for almost any situation.

The Everglades are unique. They are a horizon-spanning marshy plain, overwhelmingly flat and carpeted with grass that ripples in the wind like the largest wheat field you have ever seen. But it is not wheat. It is saw grass, which, as its name suggests, can cut you to the bone. Underneath the grass, there is water, which starts its journey in the lakes and rivers that rise as far north as Orlando and Okeechobee and which creeps down the tableland of south Florida.

Although the Everglades still appear enormous and untouched, they are being tamed and diminished. They've channeled them and drained them, burnt them and built on them. They've run highways through their green grassy heart. For now though, they are still home to multitudes of bass who can be convinced to take a fly.

I have always thought that Jack is partial to bass because he is a native Ozarkian from eastern Oklahoma who fished the White and the Buffalo Rivers back in the 1930s, before the big dams. It was, and is, great bass country. He caught his first bass on a Hawaiian Wiggler using a steel

pole, and an ivory-handled casting reel that had belonged to his grandfather. He sat at the knee of the great river guide Elmo Hertz, and he heard tales of Zane Gray and his float trips for smallmouths. After he saw Florida for the first time, he packed in his desk job and headed for the Bahamas, where he guided and ran a bonefish camp in the 1950s. "I probably caught 20,000 bonefish on a glass rod and my old Pfleuger Medalist," he says of his island days. "It got to a point, that I didn't care if I ever caught another bonefish. I was bonefished out. But bass, on light tackle, in pure surroundings . . . I don't believe I will ever tire of that."

In the thirty years that I have known him, the Everglades have helped to fulfill that bassing urge. Together, Jack and I have fished there with topwater plugs and the no-bail spinning rigs that Jack has preferred since the late 1940s. We have fished plastic worms with old Penn Senators. But mostly we have fished with fly rods and popping bugs. Jack reveres the memory of E. H. Peckinpaugh, father of the popping bug, or at least of Peck's Poppers. Jack's old johnboat is even named "Father," which is how he thinks of Old Man Peckinpaugh. "Not too many people combine fly fishing and bassing. He is the man who got me started," Jack told me. "I think bugging is such a satisfying way of fishing. Forget about all that pound-for-pound and inch-for-inch

stuff. I don't care all that much about the fight. I get excited by the take, and there is nothing like the topwater take of a bass."

Jack is what I would call an angler's angler. If you follow the magazines, you are much more likely to have heard of Lefty Kreh, or Dave Whitlock, or Doug Swisher. But every one of these legends has heard of Jack and fished with him. To me he is a man who is purely devoted to fly-fishing, but he is anything but a fly-fishing geek. His easy Ozarks drawl, his hipster's love of jazz, his old sunbleached cars, and most of all his unquenchable enthusiasm all go down easy. With other fishing guides there is always a moment of territoriality where the guide gauges how far he or she can go before treading on the client's ego. With Jack his disarming friendliness puts even the most type-A angling client at ease.

"Uh, Pete," he will say, "sometimes if you wait a little longer on the backcast I find the line loads the rod better." And then, ten minutes later, when you are repeating the same error, he will say, as if he had just noticed something for the first time, "Uh, Pete, I was watching your backcast and you just let it unroll another second or two, you're going to get a lot more distance." And then, the next time I fish with him it will be the same observation totally de novo. After all these years, whenever I find myself rushing my cast when I am using big rods and heavy lines, I hear Jack's voice, as if there were a very laid-back

Ozarks fishing genie on my shoulder. I slow down, just like the genie says, always to the benefit of my cast.

The fishing, of course, is what led me to Jack nearly thirty years ago, but the company kept me coming back. When you see Jack after a long hiatus, he picks up the conversation as if you had left him five minutes ago. He will talk about fish, flies, lines, and casting for as long as you let him. You can choose to participate or just let him go and, believe me, he keeps up his end of the conversation. In distinction to many fishing blowhards, Jack's thoughts are invariably interesting, at least to other fishermen. When my wife is along for the ride, she marvels at how much we can find to say on the subject. Or we talk about jazz. Jack is a jazzbo, a man of his times. Had he been of my generation, no doubt he would be that way about Dylan or the Rolling Stones. But at nearly twenty years my senior, jazz—cool jazz, bebopping Coltrane, Getz, and Parker jazz—was the way he got his hip card punched. Although it is

a form of music I love, I don't think about it much. To Jack it is very alive and contemporary, and you cannot avoid sharing his enthusiasm. When his cassette player works (less than even odds) we turn up the music as we trailer his old johnboat down deserted access roads in search of a "hot canal."

The Everglades, in their Army Corps of Engineers incarnation, are crisscrossed by a series of canals that are drawn down or filled up according to flood-control calculations that government managers make. When the canals are down, the bait is in the canals and the bass follow. To find such prime water, there are days that we have boated twenty miles, portaged, and motored some more. We have kept some of our catch to trade with one of the local Miccosukee Indians in exchange for passage onto their tribal lands (this was before it was discovered that the sugar industry was largely responsible for heavy levels of mercury in Everglades largemouth).

We have driven clear across the state at four in

the morning, if that's what it took to hit the right canal at the right time. The rewards have been huge. First the solitude; although the Glades teem with fish, most anglers prefer to go offshore for sailfish and marlin or down to the Keys for bones and tarpon. The reasoning must be something like, "you don't come all the way from Cincinnati or Syracuse to fish for the same bass you can find at home."

But there is more to the Glades than fish. One of the pleasures of fishing with Jack is that he knows his birds, and he announces their flight like a good baseball announcer: he tells you the whole story, but he doesn't rush it—and he doesn't overwhelm you with details. He just sits back like a man rocking on his porch on a hot day, pointing out the passing traffic. "There's a night heron coming on duty," he will say. Or, "By God, look at that kite!" referring to the hawklike bird that subsists solely on the green apple snail of the Southeast. Or he might offer similar praises for the coots, ducks, egrets, gallinules, bitterns, ravens, vultures, martens, osprey, and graceful storks of the Glades.

And then there are the gators. Where many visitors to the Sunshine State count themselves lucky if they see one gator or two sunning by some water hazard on a golf course, there are days when we have floated past two hundred gators of all sizes sunning themselves on the bank.

Finally, Jack will put you on fish. He is not, by nature, a trophy hunter. If he were, he would fish plastic worms for lunkers. He is a bass-bugger the way some trout fishermen are dry-fly fishermen to the exclusion of nymphs, streamers, and wets.

"There is nothing like a visual take," he will say by way of explanation. "I go for the action over the size every time," he will add as a postscript to his having unhooked a bass for a client. "Small but wiry," he often observes in the manner of an Ozarkian W. C. Fields.

We have had our share of good days, spectacular days, and lousy days, although a cocktail at some raucous bar cum pool hall frequented by Seminoles could always be counted on to cure the blues brought on by so-so fishing. On the other hand, there was never a day like the one that Jack and I spent way back in the Big Cypress with my daughter, Lucy.

Jack had recently lost his own Lucy, his wife of four decades, and the sadness showed on his face. I figured that having a real live Lucy on board might be a tonic for him, and it was. The angling spirits must have concurred because the fishing was so good it was downright stupid. Every cast caught a fish. For my Lucy, whose maiden bass voyage this was, it presented angling's most charitable face. I cautioned her that "real life" wasn't like this. Nevertheless, we weren't complaining about our good luck.

Just for jollies, we decided to count the number of fish caught for the next ten minutes. We put Lucy in charge of unhooking to help speed things along. At the end of the exercise we had caught and released thirty-one fish! Jack started to do the math but had trouble getting past uncontrollable laughter as he realized that, fishing in this manner, it would have been a two-thousand-bass day!

I think part of the reason we didn't keep up the pace is no one would have believed us.

BRONZED BASS

———◆———

Blackening fish is one of the finer cooking inventions of the last few decades. Paul Prudhomme, who is originally from the heart of Cajun country, is credited with inventing this technique. Although it is simple, unless it's done right, it is a perfect way to take good food and make it bad. And even then the cook must beware; although you may prepare the fish properly, the cloud of peppery smoke can fumigate the neighborhood.

James Graham, the great fish-and-game chef of Lafayette, Louisiana, came up with an alternative. He calls it Bronzed Fish, and it is one of the easier recipes that have come my way, proving that simpler is often better. Instead of blackened, the fish is reddened, using the same spices called for in blackened fish. You can use any white-fleshed fish for this technique. The result is a beautiful red-gold crust of powerful spices. In honor of Prudhomme I first tested this recipe on some largemouth bass that I caught in Two O'Clock Bayou with one of his cousins, the owner of a bait shop and fishing store outside Lafayette.

I have grown fond of bronzed fish with just a squeeze of lemon at the end. Graham made it for me with this rich and delicious sauce that is great with any fried or grilled fish. If you want to make it really easy, you can buy premixed blackening spices in many stores.

Serves 4

Blackening Spice Mix

1 teaspoon onion powder
¾ teaspoon dried oregano
¾ teaspoon dried thyme
1 teaspoon freshly ground black pepper
1 teaspoon freshly ground white pepper
1 teaspoon cayenne pepper
2 teaspoons salt
4 teaspoons paprika
1 teaspoon garlic powder

Cajun Crab Cream

2 8-ounce bottles clam juice
1 teaspoon salt
¼ teaspoon cayenne pepper
¼ cup diced onion
1 teaspoon all-purpose Cajun seasoning
(if not available combine salt, sugar,
cayenne pepper, black pepper, and
granulated garlic powder to taste)
6 tablespoons unsalted butter
2 tablespoons all-purpose flour
¼ cup heavy cream
1 cup poached shellfish
(crab, shrimp, or scallops)

Bronzing the Fish

Corn, peanut, or olive oil for frying
4 white-fleshed fish fillets (such as
largemouth, smallmouth, redfish,
blackfish, weakfish, snapper, dolphin)

Combine all the seasonings in a small bowl and set aside.

Bring the clam juice to a boil in a medium saucepan over high heat.

Add the salt, cayenne, onion, and Cajun seasoning.

Boil for 10 minutes and strain.

Meanwhile, to make the roux melt 3 tablespoons of the butter in a small skillet over medium-low heat.

Add the flour and cook for 3 minutes, or until it turns golden.

Return the strained liquid to the pot; add the remaining 3 tablespoons butter, the cream, and poached shellfish, and stir with a whisk or wooden spoon.

Thicken the sauce with 2 tablespoons of the roux.

Keep the sauce warm until you bronze the fish.

Rinse the fillets and pat them dry.

Dredge in the spice mix.

Cover a large sauté pan with ⅛ inch of oil and heat over medium-high heat.

When the oil is good and hot but not yet smoking, fry the fillets 2 to 3 minutes on each side (rule of thumb: 10 minutes cooking per inch of thickness).

If you fold over the thin tail of the fillet so that the whole piece is of uniform thickness, you will avoid ending up with a dried-out end.

Remove the fillets from the heat and transfer to serving plates.

Spoon Cajun Crab Cream over the fish, and serve.

MONTAUK

Down from the Mountains and On to the Sea

———◆———

Though I will always treasure the mystery and beauty of trout, as the years go by, I spend more time on the salt and less time on the stream. In this I am not alone. Since World War II, wintertime fly fishermen have pursued bonefish, tarpon, and permit on the tidal flats of the Keys and the Bahamas. Northeasterners as well as West Coasters began taking stripers on the fly with some regularity in the last twenty years or so. Still, the deep lore and mystique of fly-fishing were commonly held to belong solely to the salmonids.

Credit the growth in saltwater fishing to the fly-rod boom, engendered in part by Robert Redford's film version of *A River Runs Through It*. It looked so romantic, so cool. It had a New Age, Zen component combined with the excitement of the chase. Lest you feel too guilty about it, you could have the primitive thrill of a blood sport and you could very morally release your trout to grow up again. Sometimes, I think if fly-fishing hadn't been around in the mid-1980s someone would have invented it before the decade was out because it fit the cultural bill so well. With the growth in popularity, though, blue-ribbon trout streams became more and more crowded until finally, fly fishermen (and increasing numbers of fly fisherwomen) forsook the long drives to crowded streams full of fly-wary trout. In steadily increasingly numbers, they opted instead for the fish in more nearby and less crowded salt water.

My career as a saltwater fly fisherman began at a fish store on the East End of Long Island. I went to buy clams to roast with fresh-picked corn down on the beach that evening. Beth Harris, with whom I had hunted birds some years before, was cooking behind the counter.

We greeted each other with the warmth of old friends and immediately began to talk fishing. "I have a friend," she said, "Jim Clark, who fishes out in Gardiner's Bay with a fly-rod."

I called Jim, who was at that time an East Hampton schoolteacher (he is now retired). He stands six feet four, and has spent years canoeing and kayaking off Montauk (no mean feat) and making extraordinarily detailed dollhouses with windows that go up and down and doors that open and close.

I met him at his boat mooring in Three Mile Harbor, near Montauk. Jim had a twenty-three-foot Mako that he shared with another newly converted, school-teaching saltwater fly fisherman, Peter Minnick of Mill Neck. That first afternoon, we made our way across the sheltered waters of Gardiner's Bay and headed for Cartwright Shoal, which was sculpted into its present shape by the killer hurricane of 1938. Cartwright Shoal is a long, long, rocky bar, where blues, stripers, and sometimes albacore wait in the shallow current for the baitfish that the tide pushes over the shoals. I had a six-weight trout rod and a Clouser Minnow. I took the bow. Peter had the stern, and Jim, standing in the middle, threaded his casts between ours. We caught 3- to 4-pound blues all through the autumn afternoon. For a stream angler, to take a 3-pound fish on a fly in the salt was a great thrill. To have a fish that actually took line—and backing!—this was an even more life-changing triumph.

Since that first October afternoon, I have returned to the East End as often as I can. What looked at first to be an undifferentiated and unreadable expanse of water has, just like a good trout stream, revealed itself to be a place that the angler can study, understand, and sometimes predict. I have learned and studied from many masters, and since there were so few fly-rodders in the beginning, I learned as much from conventional tackle anglers as from any other source. Take Sam Lester, a sixth-generation Bonacker (as the descendants of the original settlers are known, in recognition of their roots in the town of Acobonack). He fishes two hundred days a year and has done so since his boyhood in the 1930s. He is a deft and serious angler who prefers the one-piece custom-made glass rod that is the weapon of choice among traditionalists. It is soft and buttery, with a long cork handle and no reel seat (you tape your reel on at an appropriate spot). It will throw a plug or spoon in a lazy arc and deposit it with a *chunka chunk* that I have come to associate with the sound of a bass or a bluefish about to be caught.

Sam is a surf fisherman. I met him through Josh Feigenbaum, who had fished with him for years. They made an interesting odd couple: Josh the hard-driving media mogul and Sam the quiet local. Both loved to fish more than just about anything, and that was a sufficient basis for a bond that developed into a strong friendship over the years.

Josh and I often showed up at Sam's house in late afternoon. He would be finishing his early dinner, not in a rush. We would climb into his eight-cylinder four-wheel drive and motor through Amagansett, past Clam Bar, where you can buy great fried everything, and listen to Ry Cooder tapes. We'd turn left and make our way to Napeague, where since Indian times the rocky shore had been paralleled by the poles of a line of fish traps. They intercept the schools of bait that larger predators follow as the outgoing tide sweeps the shoreline.

When the Napeague shore is in the lee, it is perfect for fly casting. The surf is much gentler than on the south-facing beaches. Early on I noticed that Sam did well with plugs, so I fished a blue-and-white popper that looked like a plug. On good days I was rewarded with bluefish and stripers erupting to engulf my fly. I was greatly indebted to Sam for showing me a place to escape wind and waves and where I could wade into the great big ocean and catch a fish on a fly.

On those early trips with Sam, Josh and I were the only fly-rodders. On the wide, white south beaches, I never saw a fly rod. In fact, I didn't think that you could do much with one in the heavy pounding surf. Although if I had stopped to think about it I would have reflected that the real sharpies all rigged a small bucktail streamer in addition to larger plugs and spoons.

On Thanksgiving weekend of my third season on the East End, Clark called me as I was staring at my computer screen. "Big stripers at Georgica," he said, "right off the jetty. Get out here."

I covered the ninety miles from my home in Brooklyn in very good time. We drove to the jetty at Georgica Beach in Jim's weather-worn truck, which presented a pleasing contrast to the beach-hugging billionaire homes of the Hamptons smart set. The surf was high and roily, almost brown. It looked about as fly fishable as a parking lot.

"You've got to be kidding, Jim," I said.

"They're there. Get out on the rocks and cast."

On my first cast, the fly that I sent forth with very little faith found its way into the mouth of a big bass.

He took me well into the backing. I eased off the jetty and out onto the beach, running forward as the breakers retreated and backward when they advanced, fighting my fish all the while. I beached him and released him, 36-inches of shivering silver.

That afternoon Jim, Peter Minnick, and I caught nine keepers, an absolutely staggering number of great fish. Meanwhile the conventional fishermen stood there heaving heavy metal into the heaving surf. They caught nothing. Fly-fishing, I realized, is not only possible in the surf, sometimes it's the very best way to fish.

LORDS OF THE FLY:
Paul

---

*S*ometimes the greatest discoveries come to those who close their ears to the common wisdom and open their eyes to what is happening all around them. That's how Paul Dixon came upon sight-casting to striped bass.

When Dixon, a California transplant, arrived in these waters, he had very little experience with stripers. He had not been raised with the grizzled old Montauk striper sharpies, who, given the slightest opportunity, would be happy to tell you: "You can't catch stripers in the daylight. Waste of time. Dawn, dusk, or the middle of the night."

This didn't jibe with Dixon's experience when he took his father-in-law's boat out during weekday afternoons, which were the only times he had use of it. He would drift over the white-bottomed tidal flats and watch big striped bass lazily cruising the shallows. They weren't supposed to be there. Could it be they were there all along and nobody had bothered to look for them?

Something must have been in the air, because shortly after he made those first observations a guy came into the fly-fishing store that Dixon owned in East Hampton. "I was up on this cliff and it was unbelievable. Right in the middle of the day I looked down and there were thousands of fish flashing in the water," the angler reported.

Dixon was stoked. "I went there the next day to check it out," he said, "and sure enough right there in the middle of the day there were thousands of striped bass. According to everything I had learned they shouldn't have been there, but there they were. The next day I went at low tide and saw that the fish were cruising over a shallow white sandy bottom, just like a flat in the Keys."

Dixon set about applying his knowledge gained while stalking bonefish and tarpon to seeking out stripers and bluefish, and in so doing, he helped to popularize a new fishery that caught on with anglers who were fascinated with this newly minted fly rod experience.

It was years before I caught what I would call a perfect flats striper under perfect conditions.

It was worth the wait.

On an early June day we pulled out of Three Mile Harbor. Overhead, bare wisps of clouds flitted across an otherwise unbroken blue vault. Within a minute of leaving the dock, Dixon hesitated for a moment and turned left.

He picked up his pole and scanned the water. "This is the prettiest flat, there's no boat traffic stirring up the fish yet, so give it a try."

Now every angler knows that in order to get good fishing you have to drive far, paddle far, walk far. It's part of the deal. So of course I held out no hope for this maneuver and stared dreamily in the middle distance munching on a Hershey bar with almonds when Dixon, sotto voce, interrupted: "Nice fish, thirty feet, three o'clock!"

I sent a backcast to a green ghost of a fish cruising along the line where the white sandy shoal turned to a ribbon of sea grass. Its dark fringe was not grass, though, but schools of wriggling sand eels no longer than your finger. Great striper bait.

"You landed in back of him," Paul admonished. As he spoke, the fish turned, opened its mouth, wide and white, and took my fly. He streaked across the flat, and I let him run until he tired: 30 inches, an auspicious start.

At this time of year the striped bass, newly arrived at their summer feeding grounds from their winter homes in the Chesapeake, Delaware, and Hudson, are hungry and eminently fishable with a fly, especially on clear tidal flats. Seeing the striper, approaching it without alarming it, and getting one, or at most two, casts off before it is alerted is an experience that combines finesse and stealth.

Once outside the harbor we poled the flats at either side of the entrance. We saw fish materialize out of the depths—like familiar faces seen for just a second in a fleeting dream. The incoming tide, nearing flood, made it hard to reach the fish before they saw us. By the time the fly could sink to their level, they were on to our game. Damn! Big fish, lots of them, but we could do no more than window shop.

Dixon decided to run west, where the tide was less advanced. The wind dropped, the sun rose, and I thought that finally I had primo conditions. But with absolutely no chop on the water, the glare made it hard to see. Paul spotted some fish, but I had trouble seeing them. It was not until I finally was able to see one on another cast that I truly wired into the flats game.

Forty feet out the fly landed in front of three fish. One of them turned!

"Leave it," Paul said, "now strip, strip." The fish followed. "Leave it." The fish came to the fly. "Now tease him hard, strip strip strip, and leave it." The striper, its predatory instincts challenged, pounced on the fly before it could "escape." It was a decent fish, not great, but instructive.

We poled the flat, miles of it. The dark shadows that had been indistinguishable when I first saw them in the morning now looked more like fish than grass

or rocks. Fish move, grass and rocks don't. The bait, like clouds moving across the sky, drifted past us, tens of thousands of shimmering sand eels. On the shore the plovers piped and squeaked and squawked. We moved into a school of fifty bass, then another, then another. Where to cast first? The amount of opportunity stymied me and left me flailing. I lit a cigar and sat down in the hot still air.

Paul spoke in a low conspiratorial tone: "Alright Pete, at 5:30, eighty feet, coming towards us. I am going to turn the boat to give you a forehand shot."

He pivoted the boat on his push pole. "When you think you have it, take it. Lead him."

I pulled on my double haul, cast into the shallow water, where three shapes moved parallel to the shore.

One of them turned. I stripped. He followed. I stopped. He charged. I stripped and stopped two more times, and he was on my fly like a linebacker on a quarterback.

"Good fish, don't try to stop him," Paul counseled. The striper ran around in a circle. I had to pass my rod around Paul's legs as I followed his course. After a splendid fight, a fourteen-pound bass came to hand. I unhooked him and watched him melt back onto the flat: alive and present one second, gone the next.

In France, every time I have a meal I am convinced it is the best one ever. I am like that with good fish, too. But after hoping for so long, to entice a fine fish and watch the contest play out before my eyes from cast to release . . . that's going to be hard to top. Très bien.

BLACK HOLES

———◆———

For a number of years I received calls from friends on the East End describing bass blitzes that were "outrageous" or "unbelievable" or "mongo." I wrote this off to guide hyperbole. I may have done this, in part, because I was pissed that I wasn't there, but even angling writers can't always drop everything and go fishing. There were a few years in a row when everything seemed to pile up in October, and I was chained to my desk.

October, in every boy's psyche (and in the psyche of everyone who ever was a boy), is World Series time. It turns out that the bass look at it that way too. There are few times when things are a lead pipe cinch, but I would say that if you wanted to bet on a day of great striper fishing on a fly, then somewhere between the fourth week of September and Columbus Day would be the time, and Montauk would be the place.

The proximity of the Gulfstream on the east serves to hem in migrating sea life. The coast of North America on the west completes a gigantic funnel whose narrowest part is Montauk. All of the animals moving south must turn at Montauk. At this same time, the bay anchovies that have matured in the estuaries and bays leave for southern parts. The bass, albacore, and blues that are likewise southward bound will hang around and grow fat on anchovies until cold weather pushes the bait out.

A few things have to go right for the confluence of bait, bass, and anglers to occur. First the south shore of Long Island must be spared the full force of hurricane season. A big blow from the south scours out sandbars and roils the waters, leaving migrating fish with few havens

and low visibility. Likewise, the less publicized but no less destructive nor'easters that come with the changing seasons can blow the bait far out to sea. Where the bait goes, the gamefish follow.

But most of the time the East End manages to evade these twin knockout punches, and the migrations of the fall pause for easy pickings and a rest when they get to the Point.

This brings me to the phenomenon I came to call the Black Hole. This is different from the garden-variety bass blitz, which also entails fish busting on the surface with gulls and terns diving into their midst in hopes of snaring bait. As with the Black Hole of the astronomer, in the Black Hole of the bass everything appears to be drawn into a vortex. It is unrelenting carnage. The sound of feeding bass is like a winter wind rattling the trees. The gulls band together in such tight masses that you wonder how they manage to flap their wings without hitting their brethren.

As with many of my experiences at Montauk, Paul Dixon had a hand in introducing me to the Black Hole. It was an October afternoon in the late 1990s. The bass had been going good for a few days and were eating predictably two hours into the tide at Caswell's Point, which is an outcropping that may once have been the farthest extension of the Montauk Headlands some thousands of years ago. The talus, or outfall, of its sandy, rocky cliffs creates fish-attracting swirls and seams in concert with the push and pull of the tides. A deep crescent, just under the cliff, is a spot ideally suited for bass to herd their bait, and then, like a haul seine that traps fish in its closing net, the bait becomes more and more concentrated until it is a writhing ball, a Medusa's head of panicked little fish.

I first saw the Black Hole with Paul and his client Gordie Hill—a physician and celebrated tarpon hunter from Big Pine Key, Florida. On our first outing, the predicted light winds and calm seas had become a stiff breeze and 4- foot seas (which, I remind the freshwater angler, means waves that measure eight feet from peak to trough).

We left Montauk Harbor and headed along the north shore to the Point, looking for blitzes along the way. Bass, albacore, blues—it didn't matter. At the beginning of every fishing day at Montauk you are convinced you will have all three and that the difficulty of the day will be choosing which species to pursue.

We didn't have much of a choice. The blues were absent and the albies were desultory when they showed at all, and they did not show often. A voice came over the radio. It was Ernie French, another of the Montauk guide corps.

"Paul . . . number eight."

It was a code that Dixon and his colleagues had worked out to designate bass hot spots.

"We're on the way," Paul shot back.

As we moved to the spot, which turned out to be Caswell's, the birds were out in force but flying lazily, dipping, climbing again. The unfocussed flight of the birds was the action of gleaners looking to pick up the little fish parts that remained after the last onslaught of bass. It all had the look of a place where something had happened . . . or was about to happen.

We waited, and looked, and waited some more. And then I saw It. In the depths, a stain darkened the water. It grew and darkened even more. At the same time it started to ascend, and as it did, its blackness took on a reddish tinge—dark red, like pooled blood. All through this very long moment there was little sound. Just the breakers piling against the shore with a long whoosh.

Then, in a split second, the tableau ruptured as the red cloud—massed rainbait—broke the surface, followed almost immediately by thousands of striped bass. Head and tail, they porpoised with mouths agape as they inhaled gobs of little fish. There were so many stripers packed so tightly that the overall impression was one of blackness as all of their stripes melded into a heaving, ravenous shadow pushing toward the shore.

It was perilous water, broken up by jagged boulders. Paul would edge along the backside of a breaking wave, leaving time for one, at most two, long casts. We tied on Clouser Minnows: their lead eyes carried them down into the marauding stripers' field of vision. Each time a striper took, Dixon backed out while we fought our fish. Hill, a mild-tempered and expert angler, was an excellent partner. Given the swells on the ocean, the pounding of the close-breaking waves, the swirling wind, and the furious maneuvers of bait and the stripers that decimated them, we had to co-ordinate our casts and, then, when we hooked up, we had to coordinate our fights, following our fish fore and aft, passing rods around one another.

For two hours, the melee continued, and we were as maddened by the riotous event as were the gulls and the bass. If you ever doubted that love of fishing comes from a deep hunter's instinct, fighting bass in the Black Hole will set you straight.

In the years that followed I made it my business to be at Montauk at the peak of the run. I even spent the month of October there one year, fishing all day every day and writing my book *The Moon Pulled Up an Acre of Bass.*

I recall one other event from that day with Paul and Gordie, equally iconic of the angler's world.

When we reached the dock, a dozen or so of the guides milled around after dropping off their clients at the Montauk Lake Club. We grabbed a bite, trading stories of the day's incredible action. Sam Talarico, an angler and photographer, had a new saltwater fisherman's calendar that featured one of his photos. As I recall, it was a handsome and shiny albacore.

As he paged through the calendar, he paused for a moment at a picture of a very pretty girl in khaki shorts. She bent over to release a snook that she had just caught. She was an eye-catching blonde, with long tan legs.

To a man, the guides looked at the photo of the lovely girl and chorused, "Nice snook!"

BLUEFISH ARROSTO
(Baked Bluefish)

While researching a cookbook with a great young Italian chef, Fabio Trabocchi, we traveled to to his home region, Le Marche. I call it The Secret Italy because for centuries it has been hard to get to this out-of-the-way province. The towering Appenine Mountains separate it from Rome, so that you have to make a long detour to the north or south in order to get there. However, for the Greeks and seafaring people of the Eastern Mediterranean as well as coastal cities such as Venice, it was an easy boat ride. Fish cookery is well developed here. I was most interested in the way that Fabio treated mackerel, which, like bluefish, is thought of as an oily or "heavy" fish.

Serves 6

Baked Bluefish

2 bluefish mackerel
(2 to 3 pounds each),
cleaned and filleted
2 cups dry white wine, such as
Verdicchio or Pinot Grigio
2 garlic cloves
¼ cup loosely packed mint leaves
1 ⅓ cups dried breadcrumbs
1 cup extra-virgin olive oil,
plus more for massaging
the flesh of the fish
Kosher salt and
freshly ground white pepper
8 bay leaves, preferably fresh

Rinse the fillets in cold water and pat dry. In a large baking dish, arrange the fillets in a single layer skin side down.

Douse with the wine.

Cover the baking dish with plastic and refrigerate for 1 hour.

Preheat the oven to 350°F.

Place the garlic, mint, breadcrumbs, and ⅔ cup of the olive oil in the bowl of a food processor. Process for about 5 minutes, stopping occasionally to scrape the sides of the bowl. Season with salt and pepper to taste.

Remove the fillets from the marinade, pat dry, and season with salt and pepper. Massage olive oil into the flesh using a small pastry brush.

Pour the remaining ⅓ cup of the olive oil into a ceramic or heavy-bottomed baking dish large enough to hold the fillets in a single layer.

Crush the bay leaves in your hand and add them to the baking dish.

Place the fillets skin side down in the baking dish.

Cover the fillets with the breadcrumb mixture.

Cover the baking dish with aluminum foil and bake for about 20 minutes, or until the fish is opaque and the flesh is firm to the touch.

Remove from the oven and serve immediately on warm plates.

BASS EAT HERRING, MAN EAT BASS, GOOD!

———◆———

In the Bible, good and bad fortune frequently occur in seven-year cycles. On Long Island, I have found this to be true of the most humongous stripers on earth.

The first time the herring, bass, and I converged was Pearl Harbor Day (December 7, 1994). It all began with a call from Paul Dixon. "They're here," he said, his voice quivering with excitement. "If you are ever going to come, come now!"

The "they" who were "here" were the big bass, twenty pounds and up. Although I was just sitting down to a peaceful domestic scene of dinner with my wife and kids, I bolted from the table, threw my gear in a duffle, and was out the door chewing down a last mouthful of spaghetti and exiting with a quick "I'll call when I get there."

That next day, balmy for December, turned out to be the best striper fishing of the year. It was not quite as riotous as the acres of stripers devouring even more acres of anchovies in October. Nor was it as heart-stoppingly suspenseful and demanding as stalking a lone fish on the sun-bleached flats in June. Think instead of smashmouth fly-fishing: big rods, big fish. In that one afternoon within two hundred yards of Montauk Point, I caught no less than twenty-five bass and not one of them under thirty inches. Four went thirty-six plus. I schlepped a pair of them back to Charlie Palmer's restaurant Aureole on the Upper East Side. Palmer, an ex-farmboy and lifelong hunter, served me some striper sashimi with white truffles and then a roast loin wrapped in pancetta. As a food writer, I could make a case for that as my last meal on earth if I am ever asked.

For the next six years, whenever there was a lull in a fishing conversation or whenever I figured some braggart needed a comeuppance for their endless stories of Patagonian trout as big as Moby Dick or thirty-pound permit taken on hundred-foot casts, I would interject with my mega-bass tales and we were back on a level playing field. Writing about this causes me to reflect that although fishing is not, fundamentally, a competitive sport, talking about fishing sure is.

For the next seven years I prayed for return of the herring and the bass, but nor'easters, sou'westers, hurricanes, or freezing weather dashed my hopes. Six years, 362 days since my first successful attempt to fish bass during the herring run, I got another fevered phone call from Paul.

In that seventh year, 2001, the water temperatures remained unseasonably high and, with the exception of one thumper of a nor'easter in mid-October, there were no big storms to disrupt the bait and drive the gamefish away. Around Thanksgiving, anglers from the Point down to Shinnecock Canal were trading stories of twenty-five-fish days. While the surfcasters were able to reach the fish, high winds and heavy seas kept most of the boats and fly-rodders off the water until late in the season.

That's when Dixon called. I hung up and speed-dialed Josh, who begged off. "Too many things to move around," he said. Five minutes later he called back: "What the hell am I thinking of? I just blew everything off."

At 8:00 the next morning, we met Dixon in South Hampton. We moved out of the quiet waters of Shinnecock and into the ocean, where a falling tide and an east wind joined forces for a molar-rattling chop. We ran for forty minutes through the cold gray morning. In the distance, the cloud bank parted on a shimmering vista of white sand, green sea, blue sky, wheeling formations of gannets, and, most telling of all, what seemed like every pickup truck in the Hamptons parked on the beach with a line of surfcasters in front of them. Like an artillery fusillade, the surface of the sea exploded with fleeing herring and, right behind them, open-mouthed bass the size of German shepherds.

We closed and cast. Wham! Paul hooked up. Wham! I felt a jolt. Wham! Josh completed the triple-header. Within five minutes we had each landed and released fish in excess of twenty-five pounds. None of us had caught fish that big in the preceding six months. But it didn't end there. In the next hour we caught another two dozen fish, included the biggest bass I have ever taken. By Paul's estimate it was 45- inches, 35-pounds.

I returned to New York with a sore back from the pounding sea, sore arms from fighting big fish, and blistered hands from line burn. But it didn't end there.

The fish that pass by Montauk will, when conditions are right, continue on down the coast to New York City. I was exhilarated, though not surprised, when another friend and guide, Brendan McCarthy, called to report that the herring and bass brigades were in Queens, right off the Rockaways. I jumped at the chance to join him. There were very few boats left in the water at Gateway Marina. Most people had hung it up for the year. We sped past Sheepshead Bay, cut through the rip at Breezy Point, and turned east. Nothing doing and not much visibility.

The swells were building. In Brendan's light flats skiff I felt every wave. Just east of Riis Park, gannets flashed as they described wide circles and then dove, hitting the water like cannonballs.

The bass showed in short-lived but furious Black Holes. I discovered that you could use a surface fly to fish these big stripers like albacore: look for the swirl, get your fly right on it, and let it sit there. Leave it a few seconds, then strip, and Mr. Bass would usually oblige with a surface take of great savagery. For two hours we caught fish in the blessedly warm December sun. The wry but ardent McCarthy broke into a smile that appeared to start at his toes and end at his baseball hat.

I bagged the fish and drove to Daniel, the restaurant on East 65th Street in Manhattan owned by Daniel Boulud, with whom I have written a number of books. I had invited him to join the fishing, but getting a chef away from his stove addiction is always iffy. He had an idea on how to prepare the striper, however, and I took him up on his offer to cook it.

With the assistance of his sous-chef, Eddy Leroux, he boned and filleted the bass, reserving the head and tail. He dusted it with sumac (a tangy Turkish spice), fiery espelette peppers from the southwest of France, lemon zest, salt, and pepper. Then they tied the fillets into a bundle, wrapping them in fig leaves. Next they took some room-temperature sculptor's clay and wrapped the

fish again, tucking the head and tail into the clay blanket. The result looked like a whole fish swaddled in clay.

As an artful flourish, Eddy made incisions along the clay to give the effect of scales. If you do this at home, you can forgo the head, tail, and scales, but wrapping in fig leaves and clay is, I am told, quite simple. Daniel placed the fish in a 350-degree oven

and 30 minutes later presented it to a chorus of oohs and ahhs in the lounge, where I waited with my brothers and my wife, Melinda.

The waiter cracked the clay, removed it, unwrapped the fragrant fig leaves, and served my striper—sea fresh and moist, with bracing but delicate flavors—and it didn't even need a pan.

BIG CITY FISHING

"At every wharf and pier and ledge
the anglers haste for perfect sport
Along the Battery's grassy edge
Up The North River and the East
Manhattan gathered to the feast."

from "The Kingfish"
by Isaac McLellan
The American Angler, 1885

A Bass Grows in Brooklyn

On the 11th of August, 1819, the paddle wheeler Bellona, under the command of the not-yet-famous Cornelius Vanderbilt, advertised a trip that would leave from the Whitehall dock in lower Manhattan at 10:00 A.M. the following Sunday. It promised "a few hours of healthful pleasure" at a spot, about ten miles east of Sandy Hook, known as "The Fishing Banks." With this announcement, according to New York angling historian, William Zeisel, the first party boat in New York waters inaugurated a low-cost and bountiful fishery that has offered sport to generations of local anglers and that has persisted down to our own time, most notably in the small but still active fleet of day boats that moor along the quay on Emmons Avenue in Sheepshead Bay.

It was on a descendant of that ship that I launched my career as an outdoor writer. The story, which appeared in *Outdoor Life*, was called "Brooklyn, Whiting, 9 A.M." It took place on a warmish day in mid-February. Our quarry was a one-pound fish, the whiting, also known as merluzzo in the restaurants of Little Italy where I had first tasted one poached in wine and clam broth. For the record, I caught three fish that day, though I felt silly when it took two pounds of lead to hold bottom in pursuit of a one-pound fish. But in the big scheme of things in my life, I would say that much more important than the fishing writing, even more important than the fishing, was being put in touch with nature in the unlikely setting of the nation's biggest metropolis. People don't think of New York City as nature's wonderland, but once you get out on the water, it is hard to avoid. You see the city in a different, more ancient light. Each morning from April through December (the fishing months), I wake up

and look at the flag on the Brooklyn piers to see which way the wind is blowing, to see if I would want to fish out at Breezy Point, or in the back of the harbor at Great Kills, or with the regulars down at the tip of Manhattan just across from the Battery.

From the rip currents of Hellgate to the sweeping arm of Sandy Hook, New York Harbor is home to a rich and thriving array of wildlife. You will find shellfish beds south of Gowanus Creek that supplied foot-long oysters to Delmonicos in the days when Daniel Webster brought in his catch of giant Long Island brook trout. Along the Arthur Kill, the Northeast's largest colony of herons nestle peacefully in the apocalyptic jumble of the Jersey shoreline. On Deadhorse Bay, bluefish throng in the shallows that once received the remains of racehorses who were processed into glue when they ran out of the money at Steeplechase Park. In the breakwater in front of Gracie Mansion the Coast Guard warns off frustrated anglers helplessly watching churned-up bait ravaged by schools of albacore. There are swans in Raritan Bay and fluke along the Bay Ridge flats. Beneath the flame of Liberty you may find a family of harbor seals and, if you are very lucky, a pod of dolphin.

The Hudson River estuary is, in fact, a fertile and relatively clean body of water; cleaner by the year and certainly a far cry from the days when the patron saint of the harbor, Joe Mitchell, wrote (in his classic *Bottom of the Harbor*), "you could bottle it and sell it for poison." What the casual observer takes for dirty is actually the naturally plankton-rich water of the estuary. These plankton anchor a bountiful food chain that includes fluke, flounder, blackfish, weakfish, bluefish, false albacore, and the prince of them all, the striped bass, which has made a heartening comeback thanks in part to strict harvesting regulations and the improvement in water quality.

When the bait is in I don't know of a more productive fishery, and yet, like most New Yorkers, I went through much of my life without an inkling that such angling riches lay, literally, at the end of my block. It took a skunking out at Montauk to clue me in to the promise of my local waters. It started when I attempted to reciprocate on the hospitality that Argentine sportsman Carlos Sanchez had shown me on a fishing trip to Patagonia. I invited him to visit me some fall when things busted out at Montauk.

When Carlos called to let me know that he had a few days to kill on his trip to the States, I invited him out East. He could scarcely believe the riot of fish and birds going on at Montauk. Less happily, I could scarcely believe that after two days of chasing birds and running up and down the beaches we had not even cast to one fish! Nothing came close to the shore.

"Really, Carlos, it's never like this. You always catch fish," I said just as any number of guides have said to me to explain why plentiful fish disappeared just before I showed up.

We drove back to Brooklyn, where the following message awaited on my answering machine: "Peter, Nick Lyons said you might be interested in this. The fish are stacked like cordwood right off of Manhattan. And you can catch fish until you are tired and still be in the office by 10 A.M."

The caller was Gary Sherman, a member of a family of New York doctors all of whom are gonzo fishermen. Carlos gave a "what the hell?" shrug, and the next morning we met the Shermans at Caesar's Bay (between Coney Island and The Narrows). Within minutes of leaving the dock, we were into a blitz of cocktail blues, as three-pound fish are locally known.

But blues were not part of the Sherman master plan. Bass were. We ran the Brooklyn Shore and pulled up just off the Manhattan slip for the Staten Island ferry. Their old family friend, Dominic, aligned the boat by referring to some secret landmarks, and we drifted over a little hole in Diamond Reef just north of Castle Clinton. During the next half hour we caught fish after fish, all of them big. Carlos was now a believer, and I became, henceforth, a Big Apple angler.

I have written about New York City fishing ever since and caught many fine fish. Nothing gave me greater satisfaction, though, than a call I received one afternoon while I was at my desk, writing.

"Is this Peter Kaminsky?" the voice said in the genteel drawl of the Carolinas.

"It is."

"Well, this is Joe Mitchell."

I caught my breath. Apart from his definitive work on New York Harbor, Mitchell had been my absolute number-one idol as a nonfiction writer ever since my Dad gave me a copy of *McSorley's Wonderful Saloon*.

"I've been reading your stories about the harbor," he said referring to a series I had done that year in the *New York Times*. "It was like a postcard from an old friend."

"Joe," I answered, "coming from you, that is about the highest praise I ever had."

"Why don't we get together for lunch in the New Year?" he asked.

"Sure," I said, but with travel and deadlines I let the winter slip away. And then one day I read his obit in the paper. I have since resolved never to be too busy.

IN THE NARROWS

———◆———

*A*t the tip of the Rockaway Peninsula, on the bay side of Breezy Point, there is a long, gently sloping beach where the daily cycle of the tides brings schools of stripers and blues to feed. If you are a surface fisherman, and I am, one of the delights of this spot is that you can track the progress of your fly (or plug) in the carnival lights of Coney Island, between the tall umbrella-like spire of the Parachute Jump and the huge circle of the Ferris Wheel. You are sheltered from the prevailing sea breezes so that casting conditions are almost ideal. Over the years I have taken some fine fish in the rip right in front of the Parachute Jump.

Dave Taft, a senior park ranger at the Jamaica Bay Wildlife Refuge, is an artist and lifelong angler. He hails from Canarsie, the traditional jumping-off spot for the Rockaways. In the 1860s, when New Yorkers first took up ocean bathing in great numbers, the old Brooklyn and Rockaway Beach Railroad began steamer service from Canarsie Landing to Seaside Park on the bay shore of Rockaway Peninsula. At that time a number of flat-bottomed sloops and a handful of steam-powered boats made up a prosperous fishing fleet that sold fluke, flounder, striped bass, weakfish, and blues. Oysters, planted in the spring and harvested through the fall, grew robustly in the warm shallow waters of Jamaica Bay, supporting a successful shell-fishing industry until well into the twentieth century, when a number of typhus outbreaks put an end to it.

Dave and I have surf-cast Breezy Point on the falling tide when blues and stripers hang at the edge of the channel for bait moving with the tide. It seems little like New York out there. You park in a lot maintained by the Park Service. A short walk leads you through shore grass to a small cove that ends in a point and a long sandbar. The beach stretches to your left. There are always a few fishermen who, like city fishermen all around New York, are usually pretty free with advice and invariably friendly (like you, they seem to revel in this gift of nature that offers angling solitude in the middle of Megalopolis).

Though the fishing is difficult, you do hook up from time to time, which makes for a maintenance dose of angling success. All through August, about ten years ago, Dave and I cast well into the night and sometimes until early morning. We saw fish. Even more maddeningly, we often heard them around us, splashing and feeding on everything but our flies. These things happen, and when they do, there is no recourse but to return again and again, like a gambler who keeps playing at a losing table because soon his luck has to turn.

Come fall, though, things usually pick up. And the year that Dave and I walked the beaches at night, *New York Times* photographer and fellow angler Keith Meyers offered to take me on his boat so that we would be able to reach the fish wherever they were in the area of Breezy Point. The wind was out of the north and the moon was full when Keith and I set out from Jersey City (I invited Dave to join us, but he couldn't get off early).

We moved down the West Side of Manhattan, and I suggested a detour to some of the piers on the Jersey side, where there were reports of blues crashing into schools of bunker. "No go," Keith said. "The military have closed everything. They'll fire across our bow."

That didn't sound like a low-stress side trip, so we made straight for Breezy, where a frothy rip had set up with the onset of the flood tide. Two other boats, both of them trolling, cruised back and forth across the rip. I tried a Clouser Minnow and Keith started with a Rattler on a light spinning rod. We both got a hit, but neither of us connected. We moved inside the inlet, right off the beach where Dave and I had fished. "Now I've got you cornered," I said to any bass within earshot, but they weren't listening.

The stripers had to be somewhere. Keith suggested a cruise across the Narrows. We passed Norton Point, which usually holds fish under working birds. But there were neither birds nor fish. Ditto Gravesend Bay, where schoolie bass can usually be found just off of the Toys "R" Us parking lot.

The wind had settled down and Keith liked the look of Hoffman Island, just below the Verrazzano Narrows Bridge. The rocks there usually hold bass, especially on a rising tide. Setting his stern into the direction of our drift gave me a clear right-handed cast. I tied on a popper and set it gurgling among the rocks. On the first circuit of the island I did nothing. Keith's Rattler, which ran at a depth of four feet, produced two strikes, both tentative, but strikes nonetheless. Keith asked if I wanted to try some bait, but I am serious about getting to know where and how to fish the harbor with a fly rod. It's taken me years to get this far. I switched back to a Clouser and got two short takes right away. I started to feel "in the zone" as the saying goes.

The moon had climbed halfway up the eastern sky and the *QE2* passed right under her, all white and pink in the twilight. At that moment she looked like the biggest, most stately thing in creation. A flock of mallards flew in front of us, silhouetted against the ship's hull. The birds continued up through the Narrows. Then, Keith's rod bent violently. "Good fish," he said. I dropped my rod and picked up the landing net, but Keith was fishing four-pound test, and this fish was not going to surrender any time soon. At first we thought it was a bass. Then Keith declared it was a blue. When we caught a glimpse of it we were sure it was a weakfish. Ten minutes later, it turned out to be a 9-pound bass, fresh and healthy, white as clear moonlight with bold black stripes. Keith unhooked the bass and held it in the water, guiding it back and forth to revive it after the tiring fight. Soon its strength returned, and it glided back into the harbor.

HERMAN THE GERMAN

———◆———

When asked to explain his success at the plate, Wee Willie Keeler, the five-foot-four outfielder with the New York Highlanders, said, simply and immortally, "Hit 'em where they ain't." This is an excellent philosophy for getting on base but not a very good one for fishing. New York Harbor is so big, its coastline so varied, its bottom so changing, that ninety percent of angling success is a result of "hitting 'em where they are."

On Staten Island, Herman Steiniger showed me where they are.

Herman worked at Sloan Kettering, the world-famous cancer laboratory and hospital. "I needed something to take my mind off work. Fishing does that," he told me shortly after I had started to surf-cast on the south shore of Staten Island. It is a place very fly-roddable because the protecting arms of Breezy Point to the east and Sandy Hook to the west and south keep the surf down. It certainly looked right, but I wasn't catching many fish. Then, one afternoon, while exploring a new part of the coastline, I saw Herman park his car and put on his waders in a deserted part of the lot at Great Kills. The only place he could be going was a potholed cove known as The Bogs. I had been warned not to fish there without someone who knew where the holes were.

"Mind if I follow you in?" I asked Herman.

"Be my guest," he replied.

We continued down to the water, under an old sewer pipe that extended across the cove. The tide was coming in, so we had to walk on top of the huge conduit. We could see stripers tearing through bait on the surface. They made a slashing sound. When the school came in closer, Herman cast his plug and caught a number of schoolies. They approached within fly-rod range for just a few minutes. I stripped out sixty feet of line, double-hauled really hard, and sent my popping bug flying. When a small bass took, I crossed that important existential dividing line between Places With Fish and Places With No Fish.

When the school moved off, we knocked off for some coffee and a piece of pie at a place I had grown quite fond of for après fishing. I had first stopped in there after a morning checking out the beaches with my youngest daughter, Lily. An intriguing sign said, "Kids pay 1 cent per pound." By that they meant that children, when accompanied by a parent, would be charged for their breakfasts—whether pancakes or eggs and bacon or oatmeal and hot chocolate—at the rate of one penny for each pound of body weight. By that calculation, Lily's breakfast cost 52 cents.

Herman and I paid about twice that for a piece of pie. When we parted, he said he would call me when the fishing got going in the spring.

The winter was demonic. The fish didn't come in until June was well under way. Herman phoned in early July to report that he had caught some nice bass.

At five the next morning I drove over the misty Narrows and along the South Beaches. I passed Great Kills and parked near Carmen's, an old Spanish restaurant that sits on a bluff overlooking Raritan Bay. There were gulls and terns working close to shore. To my right I saw the point of Spanish Camp, a ramshackle collection of cabins named for its original settlers (and since torn down). Beyond that lay Sandy Ground, where in the nineteenth century freed slaves had prospered in the then-bountiful oyster business supplying the saloons of Ragtime Manhattan. But when Standard Oil put in the big refineries in New Jersey, the oyster beds were poisoned and remained toxic for a century.

I walked down to the water. Herman was already fishing. I yelled to him. He gestured broadly, indicating that I should proceed very carefully. The bay was covered with slippery, toe-stubbing rocks requiring tentative baby steps. Herman hooked into a bluefish, which he fought and released. "They were in strong just when the sun came up," he said. We fished for an hour. Herman showed me the underwater paths and pitfalls of the bay. The sun was very hot. The air was sticky. The blues kept feeding furiously. We fished until they stopped hitting. The action was so good we stopped counting.

But it is another fish—the bluefish, generally held to be less glamorous than the striped bass—that is framed in my memory right next to Herman.

We were casting near a salt pond close to the Arthur Kill: Herman, me, and his buddy Ritchie Chan. Ritchie's job, monitoring shipping and traffic on the Arthur Kill, kept him at work until 4 A.M., so he always knew about the early morning fishing before anyone else did.

We were the only ones on the beach, so we spread out. The rumble of foghorns slipped in from the foggy distance, a comforting baritone. Any ocean-going ship heading up to Newark Bay has to turn into the channel by running parallel to the coast before making a sharp course correction into the Kill. For a minute I had the illusion—and the apprehension—of a huge tanker swamping me with its bow wave.

A sandbar ran along the shore, about fifteen yards from the beach. The sea was calm, rocking ever so slightly. I cast into the water that lapped over the bar and pulled the fly back into the trough between the bar and the beach so that it behaved like a baitfish washing over a shoal. I did this mindlessly, as if I were wet fly-fishing in a stream. Cast-step-cast. I much prefer seeing my quarry and targeting it, but this rarely happens with the bluefish.

Bluefish have the reputation—not entirely unjustified—of brutishness: they maul their prey. They don't take your fly because you have deceived them. They just bite whatever is within toothshot, so to speak. But if you come upon a bluefish waving its black fin as it calmly feeds, it is as wary as a trout. It needs to be approached with caution and the cast must be delicate and accurate.

As I walked along the line of the sandbar I saw two little fins waving seductively. They barely broke the surface. I stopped. I waited. Ten feet farther on, the same two fins reappeared. It was a pair of blues, moving along and eating just like two bonefish on a flat. I stripped off twenty feet of line and false cast just once: a wide lazy loop that I snapped slightly at the end of the cast to help turn over the metal-eyed Clouser. The fly plopped into the water, landing as delicately as the typically ungainly Clouser can plop. It landed five feet in front of the fish. I let it sink, and as they neared it, I began to strip it away from them (which is the same direction in which fleeing bait would move). Slowly and calmly a bluefish tracked it, tipped down, and ate. He shook his head and ran, but I knew he was mine. Even in working-class Staten Island, this most proletarian fish had found a shore of serene beauty to put on a fight worthy of Izaak Walton's daintiest trout.

MEALS: FRESH BROOKLYN BLUEFISH
with Farfalle and Oven-Roasted Tomato Sauce

———◆———

Whenever I tell non-anglers that I fish the waters of New York Harbor, I know, without fail, what the next sentence will be.

"Yikes! Can you eat them?" they ask in the mistaken belief that the harbor waters are a mixture of sludge and industrial effluent washing over the cement-jacketed victims of Mafia rub-outs.

I then assure them that New York Harbor is, in reality, part of a fjord, or long arm of the sea, whose tidal reach extends to Troy, so it is cleaned twice a day by scouring tides. Moreover, the steady improvement in water quality as a result of government regulation has resulted in fish that are, for the most part, okay for human consumption. I say for the most part because there are still some polluted areas and, in the case of striped bass, the PCBs that have lodged in the river upstate at the old General Electric plant often find their way into the adipose tissue of Hudson River stripers. For that reason, I only eat stripers that move along the south shore of Long Island or Staten Island because those fish are said to be Delaware River and Chesapeake Bay stock.

Bluefish, because they are creatures purely of the ocean, are almost always okay to eat. The problem here is that many people turn up their noses at bluefish. "Too fishy!" they say. Of course this is a statement that could be applied to any fish. I don't think "fishy" is the problem. What they are referring to is the rancid aroma that oily fish acquire after

they have been exposed to the air. This characteristic is shared, by the way, with tuna and salmon—two pricey and stylish fish.

My solution? Eat them fresh and don't expose them to the air. When eaten fresh, bluefish are not only passable, they are delicious. Moreover, they have enough flavor to complement powerhouse ingredients. And furthermore, they are a fine go-to fish, almost always catchable, and they serve as a wonderful and toothsome consolation when a striper expedition ends in a skunking.

And so it happened one June afternoon that I found myself on Jamaica Bay. My intention was to catch striped bass, but the silver-sided legions that had been there the previous few days had, apparently, snuck out overnight, like tenants skipping out on the rent.

Still, there were hordes of bunker laid up in a back bay by Runway #9 at Kennedy Airport. I don't know what it is about that particular bay, but fish seem to love it almost as much as the airport police want anglers to avoid it. The way to manage this situation is to fish until they ask you to leave. It is a real kick to be catching fish right next to a line of idling jetliners. Part exhibitionist thrill, part stolen pleasure, the pure aliveness of such angling got an exponential jolt when the pursuit of fish took you to the end of the runway just as the Concorde took wing overhead.

So there Brendan McCarthy and I were, tracking schools of blues as they penned up migrating menhaden. In the space of half an hour we had hooked up at least a dozen times, releasing eleven fish and keeping one for dinner.

The inspiration for the meal that I cooked that evening—bluefish and farfalle in a sauce of tomatoes, capers, white wine, and lemon juice—was the ineffable triglia (red mullet) and farfalle that I first sampled in a plain old fish joint on the boardwalk in Viareggio, Tuscany. Bear in mind, though, that "nothing special" in Tuscany is food to beat the band in the rest of the world.

Serves 4

Sauce

1 ½ pounds oven-roasted tomatoes (recipe follows; or you may substitute canned Roma tomatoes)
Juice of 1 lemon
2 tablespoons capers
3 garlic cloves (from the oven-roasted tomatoes)
1 teaspoon sugar
¾ cup white wine
Freshly ground black pepper

Strain the oven-roasted tomatoes and reduce in a large saucepan over high heat.
Add the lemon juice and capers, and cook for 30 seconds.
Reduce the heat to low, add the tomatoes, garlic, and sugar, and cook for 2 minutes.
Add the wine and cook 2 minutes more, or until the raw taste of the wine dissipates.
Add black pepper to taste. Don't be shy here—15 or 20 turns of the mill.
Reduce the heat to very low and keep warm while you prepare the rest of the dish.

Pasta

2 tablespoons salt
1 pound farfalle

To make the pasta, bring 2 quarts of water to a boil.
Add the salt, then the farfalle, and boil about 11 minutes, until the farfalle is soft but still al dente.

Bluefish

1 tablespoon olive oil
1 pound bluefish, cut into 2 fillets

Meanwhile: Heat the olive oil in a large skillet over high heat until very hot but not smoking. Add the bluefish and 1 ½ minutes on each side, until the fish is white all the way through.
Drain the pasta, mix in the sauce, then add the fish, breaking it into bite-size chunks.

Oven-Roasted Tomatoes

5 pounds plum tomatoes
1 tablespoon sugar
10 garlic cloves, unpeeled
3 sprigs fresh thyme
1 tablespoon fleur de sel
Freshly ground black pepper
About 1 tablespoon olive oil

Preheat the oven to 200°F. Blanch the tomatoes in a large pot of boiling water. Remove the skin, cut in half, and remove the seeds and pulp. Line 2 13 x 17-inch sheet pans with parchment paper.
Place tomatoes cut side down on the parchment and scatter the sugar, garlic, thyme, salt, and pepper over tomatoes. Roast the tomatoes for 3 hours—they should be shriveled but moist and not dried out, like sun-dried tomatoes. Depending on the tomato, you may roast for another hour.

ROCKAWAY ROCKFISH
with Salsa de La Boca

———◆———

About five years ago I was on a tour of the province of Mendoza with a bunch of wine writers. Francis Mallman (see Brook Trout with Rosti Potatoes, page 83) prepared a lunch for the Catena family, Argentina's biggest and most respected winemakers. The guest of honor was Eric Rothschild (of the famous Rothschilds, makers of the greatest Bordeaux). We drove into the mountains from the town of Mendoza and parked by a stream. Francis, who does everything with as much style and savoire-faire as Fred Astaire doing the Continental, had stationed two chic and attractive waitresses by the stream. As we piled out of the car, they reached into the cold stream and retrieved two bottles of champagne, which they uncorked and poured for us in crystal flutes. And, just in case we developed a thirst along the way to the grove where he was preparing a barbecue, more waiters and waitresses, equally elegant, waited to refill our glasses every hundred yards or so.

Finally we reached the barbecue, where Francis had covered up a whole salmon with a mound of salt. After it had been an hour on the fire, he removed the fish from the heat and broke the salt crust with a mallet. Inside, the most moist and perfectly cooked salmon awaited us, needing nothing more than an herbed, garlic-rich lemon juice and olive oil mix. Since that time I have made this same dish with striped bass, bluefish, and weakfish. If you use a big fish, this can be as dramatic a presentation as any roast.

Serves 8

Salsa

2 cups olive oil
1 cup chopped flat-leaf parsley
½ cup chopped garlic
½ cup chopped fresh oregano
Zest of 2 lemons finely diced
Sea salt
Freshly ground black pepper

Fish

8 carrots
6 medium-sized potatoes
6 sweet potatoes
5 3-pound boxes kosher salt
1 8-pound striped bass, unscaled

Combine the salsa ingredients in a medium bowl and set aside. Place the carrots on a sheet of aluminum foil and wrap tightly to make a sealed bundle. Wrap each potato and sweet potato in foil. Heat oven to 500°F degrees. Pour the salt into a very large bowl and add 8 cups water. Combine the salt and water by hand. It should have the moist consistency of spring snow. Fill a roasting pan with some of the salt and tamp down so that you have about an inch of compacted salt. Lay the fish on the salt. Lay the foil wrapped carrots on the salt, followed by the potatoes and sweet potatoes. Using the remaining salt, cover the fish and vegetables as you would if you were at the beach burying someone in the sand. Tamp the salt down firmly. It should be 1 to 1½ inches thick. Very carefully place the pan in the lower third of the oven and bake about 55 minutes, or until a meat thermometer reaches 150°F. (I keep track of the temperature by sticking a meat thermometer—not instant read—through the salt and into the fish before I place the fish in the oven.)

Remove the pan from the oven and let rest for 20 minutes. Tap the salt crust with a hammer or mallet until it cracks. Discard the salt (throw it in the sink and run water on it), and remove the vegetables. Brush the remaining salt from the fish and lift off and discard the skin.

To serve, use two large spoons to lift the fish from the backbone and transfer to serving plates. Place a serving of carrots, potatoes, and sweet potatoes on each plate. Garnish with the salsa, and serve.

What have I left out? As far as this book goes, I have included most of the places that I have seriously fly-fished. Off the top of my head, I have also fished in Georgia, Alabama, Ohio, Connecticut, Illinois, Maine, Kentucky, Massachusetts, Mississippi, and the Carolinas, but not very much or, at least, not very much with a fly rod. I still need to fish steelhead in the Northwest and smallmouth on the Boundary Waters in northern Minnesota. Texas redfish on San Padre Island, I am told, are marvelous when fought from the beach. The Green River in Utah, the White in Arkansas, and the San Juan in New Mexico are also high on my list. I'd love to catch some of the big brookies that remain in the Rapid River in Maine, and, while I am in the North Country, I could stand hooking into a landlocked salmon.

On the Great Lakes, taking lake trout during those few weeks that they are in the warm shallows would be a kick. Any place that I can convince a muskellunge to take a fly would, likewise, be terrific. Panfish are great in farm ponds anywhere. I definitely want to fish the old quarries in Thornton, Iowa, with the octogenarian mother-in-law of pig farmer extraordinaire Paul Willis: not because the fishing will be so amazing but because, as with so many fishing experiences, the people you meet are almost as important as the fish.

Mind you, I said almost.

Fundamentally, I realize that while fishing in new places is nice, the joy of fishing is not about newness. In fact it is old, one of the oldest things there is for us humans. We have always done it and will always do it. When there is no more fishing, the earth will be so wildly out of balance that there is every likelihood that there will be no more people either. In the big scheme of things, the one that sometimes reveals itself when I am standing in a stream with a rod in my hand, I know that fish and fishers are cut from the same fragile cloth.

INDEX

PHOTO CREDITS

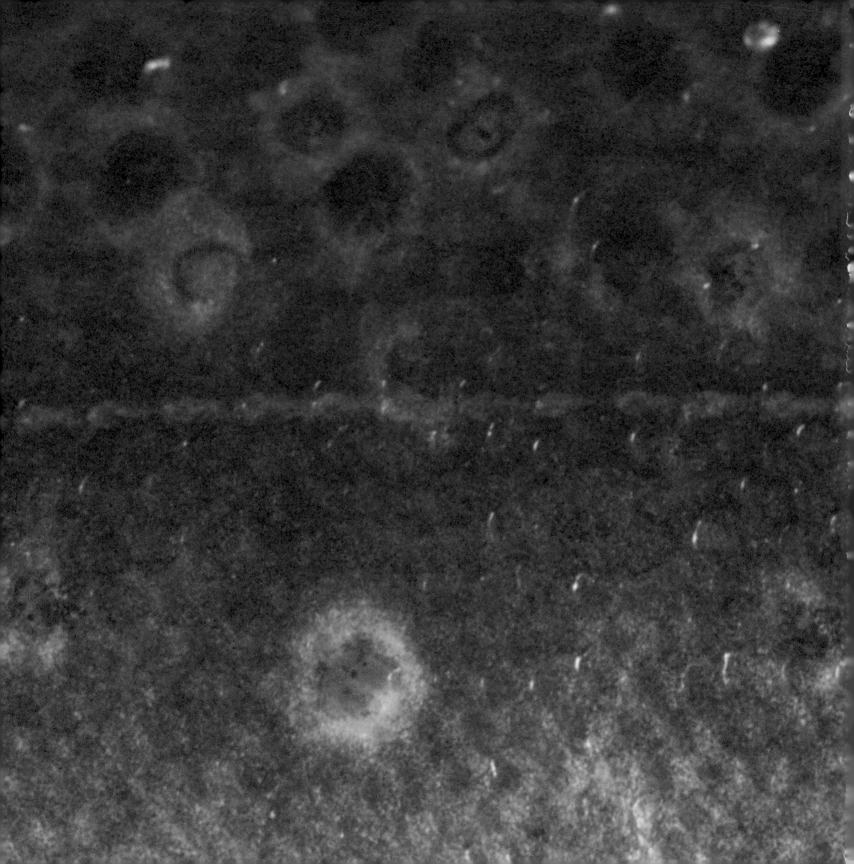